Color, like beauty, should never lick off.

Introducing
New Lick-Resistant Purrference

Purrference announces a new standard in color and flavor. With a lick-resistant breakthrough no other fur color has. Now Purrference is more than superior color and flavor — it's color that actually resists licking off.

Your color stays brighter, longer. Won't lick off. Stays true from roots to tips — even if you lick it all day, every day. And in your favorite flavors — mouse, tuna, and cream.

Because you're worth it.

Advanced Flavor Technology

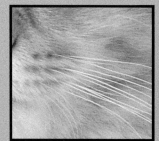

Only Purrference has patented flavor-enhancing molecules which lock in taste and resist color lick-off.

GM CONTENTS

PAGE 74: Cats' Cookbook: Easy meals for busy cats

PAGE 32: Glamour Puss: Sex kittens reveal their beauty secrets

PAGE 52: At home with America's do-it-yourself Queen, Mouser Stewart

PAGE 48: Morris: "From stray to spokescat, how I got a leg up on the competition."

GM CONTENTS

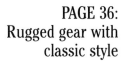

PAGE 25: Homemade catnip mice to give or to keep

PAGE 36: Rugged gear with classic style

PAGE 85: "I kept this secret all my life..."

GM INSTITUTE REPORT

PAGE 22: Scratch 'n' Sniff: Litter boxes that really work

COVER PHOTOGRAPH OF MORRIS THE 9-LIVES CAT BY DENNIS MOSNER; Styled by Ilene Hochberg; Lamé mice by L. Coffey, Ltd.; AUTHOR PHOTOGRAPH BY DENNIS MOSNER; Hair and Makeup by Jerry Ng; Sweater by Mabel's; Cat Jumpsuit by Premier.

It's fun to be The First Cat.
My favorite part is the State Dinners.
My constituents think that I get to drink as much milk as I want.
But I prefer to drink cream.
It has all the same nutrients as whole milk, with extra fat.
They don't call me a political fat cat for nothing!

CREAM

What a big fat surprise!

For More Infurmation
1-800-FAT-CATS

NOW.
SMUDGE-
PROOF.
THE
PAW
LOOK!

**Introducing
New
Pawfessional
Advanced
Smudge-proof
Mascara.**

For dramatically
long lashes
that stay that way.
All day.
No matter
how many
times you wipe
your face clean!

Anti-smudge.
Anti-smear.
Safe for
sensitive paws.

COVER CAT

Good Mousekeeping

CREATED, PRODUCED, AND WRITTEN BY:
ILENE HOCHBERG
SCHIFF!SHARFF: Art Direction/Design   SARAH SCHEFFEL: Editor
DENNIS MOSNER: PHOTOGRAPHER
MICHAEL FRAGNITO: Publisher, Penguin Studio

INSPURRATION: IRWIN HOCHBERG

PURRSONAL ASSISTANTS: NUBIE AND BARGIE HOCHBERG
CAT HANDLER: Linda Hanrahan
COPY EDITING: Judy Sandman
PHOTO ASSISTANT; PAINTED BACKDROPS: Aillinn P. Brennan
PHOTO ASSISTANTS: Roberto Cermak, Rob Houston, Kaysh Shinn
HAIR AND MAKEUP: Jerry Ng
CAT BODY DOUBLE: Wanda
PRODUCTION: Roni Axelrod, Barbara Parisi
PUBLICITY: Maureen Donnelly, Carolyn Coleburn, Karen Li, Sue Halstead

LITTERMATES: Holly Rosenthal, Joelle and Bradley Silverman, Carol Hochberg, Lindy, Seth and
Hayleigh Hochberg, Gail, Steven, Alex and Rachel Hochberg, Trudy Berhang (A.K.A. mom),
Bernard Rosenthal, Malvina and Joseph Farkas, Ellen and Ben Farkas, Miriam and Seymour Hill

FUREVER FRIENDS: Carl D'Aquino, Donna Biheller, Kim Cambell, Linda Coffey, Sue Halstead,
Dawn Haney, Phyllis Levy, Jeanne Mathews, Charlotte and Janis McAvoy, Elaine Pfefferblit,
Debra and Joe Riggio, Anya and Albert Salama, Jackie Tuttelman, Sig Zises, Nancy and Jay Zises,
and *all* the cat parents

CAT COMPANIONS: Alisha Armstrong, David and Roni Axelrod, Byron Baker, Mary S. Case,
Andrea and Melanie Cecka, Paula and Mark Chamberlin, Dawn Haney, Amy T. Hanna, Linda
Hanrahan, Jessica Hartshorn, Kimio Honda, Peter Hoppmann, Margot Horsey, David Ivizarry,
Toby Kalucki, Mimi Kayden, Elizabeth Knock, Bethlyn Krakauer, Vicky Kuehner, Phyllis Levy,
Ronald C. Longe, Dorothy Magnani, Dennis Mosner, Mike Nirenberg, Debbie J. Palmer, the
Parisis, Deborah G. Riggio, Bonnie Rosenblum, Janis S. Rosner, Sarah Scheffel, Bettina Seifert,
Cheryl Silverman, Jennifer Simon, Cari Swanson, Jacki Deena Tutelman, Philip and Sandra
Wilentz, the Zables, Jaye Zimet

TOP CATS: Abigail, Archie, Atilla, Bargie Cat, Bianca, Brandy, Bright Stars, Calico, Chaz, Coco,
Emily, Fay, Garfield, Goober, Jake, Jasmine, Katie, Kaya, Mickey Kats, Miss Kitty, Kubla, Louie,
Luna, Mew, Morris, Mouchie, Mozart, Natasha, Nyota, Oliver, Ophelia, Pansy, Po Patty, Peaches,
Pia, Quincy, Ray, Red, William Shakespeare, Socks, Spooky, Sydney Elizabeth Mehitabel Joad,
Tigger, Tinkerbell, Bailey Walsh, Wanda, Sweet William, Willie, Yin Yang, Zoey

PENGUIN STUDIO
Published by the Penguin Group
Penguin Books USA Inc., 375 Hudson Street, New York, New York 10014, U.S.A.
Penguin Books Ltd, 27 Wrights Lane, London W8 5TZ, England
Penguin Books Australia Ltd, Ringwood, Victoria, Australia
Penguin Books Canada Ltd, 10 Alcorn Avenue, Toronto, Ontario, Canada M4V 3B2
Penguin Books (N.Z.) Ltd, 182–190 Wairau Road, Auckland 10, New Zealand

Penguin Books Ltd, Registered Offices:
Harmondsworth, Middlesex, England

First published in 1996 by Penguin Studio,
an imprint of Penguin Books USA Inc.

1 3 5 7 9 10 8 6 4 2

Copyright © Ilene Rosenthal Hochberg, 1996
Photographs copyright © Ilene Rosenthal Hochberg and Dennis Mosner, 1996
All rights reserved
ISBN 0 14 02.5673 3

Printed in the United States of America

CAT SPIT.

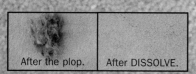

| After the plop. | After DISSOLVE. |

PREDATOR'S NOTEBOOK

Welcome to the latest issue of *Good Mousekeeping*, GM to our intimates. We take great pride and pleasure in examining life from a feline purrspective. We offer our readers the latest poop on a wide category of subjects that reflect the interests of today's housecat. From feline fashion to cat cookery, we cover the spectrum of your concerns, providing you with real infurmation on how to live well and do everything better.

Morris, The 9-Lives Cat

OUR COVER CAT IS THE unfurgettable Morris. Like many other celebrities, a single name is sufficient identification. We flew to Chicago to meet with him at his elegantly appointed office, which overlooks the city streets on which he was born. While the tape recorder whirred in the background, he related a tale of rats to riches— how a humble streetcat catapulted to the top of a large corpurration. Today his tail is held high in victory. Take a moment to paws and reflect upon his exciting life story.

IN THIS ISSUE WE WELCOME TWO NEW MEMBERS TO OUR GROWING GM FAMILY. Both are dedicated to making all of our lives more fulfilling in every way!

CONTRIBUTING PREDATOR SCRATCHING POST COMES FROM a proud heritage of GM predators. Her human companions have written for this publication for longer than anyone can remember, so she is the purrfect choice to continue our petiquette column. Please send your letters and questions to her at our office.

Contributing Predator Scratching Post

Contributing Predator Petty Noonan

PETTY NOONAN IS MAKING HER debut as contributing predator in this issue as well. Ms. Noonan, the mother of a young kitten, has been a political insider, and was the special assistant and speech-writer for Morris the Cat in his recent leap for the Purresidency. A best-selling pawthor, Ms. Noonan will write a monthly column called "Looking Furward." The column will focus upon the values, dilemmas, and rewards of feline life. We hope you'll enjoy her purrsonal miews on this pet subject.

Feline Levine

The Spray
Cat's Pajamas

CHATILLY

BREEDERS' LETTERS

Kate Mouse

I was very interested in reading about model Kate Mouse. You see, I am of slender build. Cats always assume that I am deliberately trying to keep my weight down. I, too, have been wrongly accused of being anorexic or bulimic, when in fact my body shape is hereditary. I can't help it if I have a fast metabolism or if I lead an active lifestyle, which burns calories. I just think that fat cats are jealous that they can't be as thin as I am. When I was growing up, the other cats in the neighborhood made fun of me and made me self-conscious of my looks. It was good for me to read about another cat who experienced a lot of the same things that I did. Thanks, Kate, for being true to yourself and for finding a career path that celebrates that difference. I'll hold my head up high, following your example.

Stringbean
Elmer, NJ

Hooked on Catnip

Your recent article on the horrors of catnip addiction, *Social Nipping: How to Tell if Your Kitten is Hooked on Catnip,* was enlightening. I am the mother of three kittens, who live with me at home. Two of them use catnip in responsible quantities. My third kitten, however, seems to have a problem in knowing his limits. He abuses catnip and is often found wandering the yard in an aimless and delirious state. Your article made me recognize the signs of trouble in my own youngster. I was able to seek the help of my people in eliminating all catnip, and catnip-filled toys, from my home. My kitten has returned to normal behavior. I can't thank *Good Mousekeeping* enough for alerting me to this serious problem that was occurring right under my nose.

Potpurri
Queens, NY

Cat Sup

I enjoyed trying the delicious recipes you included in your recent food feature, *Cat Sup.* It never occurred to me to add ketchup to canned cat food! Yummy! Made it taste just like the meat loaf Mamma used to make. Thanks for bringing back such warm memories.

Precious Pi
San Antonio, TX

There's just one word for your recent article, *Cat Sup* — delicious! I devoured the whole article, page after page. Poured ketchup right on the pages and lapped it up! I've always found *Good Mousekeeping* to be in the best of taste; this article certainly proves it to me! Keep up the good work. I can hardly wait to read, and taste, a feature on dessert.

Peaches
Kintnersville, PA

Julia Ropurrts

Whatever happened to that cute kitten, Julia Ropurrts? We'd heard that she disappeared after her recent divorce, and until your recent interview with her, her fans, myself included, had no idea of what had become of her. We're delighted to see that she's back, appearing in a guest spot with that heartthrob Matthew Purry on TV. Julia, we can't wait to see you in your next picture. Welcome back!

Smudgy
Phoenix, AZ

Andie McMeowell

It was so much fun to visit with Andie McMeowell and her litter of kittens at home on the ranch. I found it a refreshing surprise to see one of my favorite movie stars, who I picture as a real sophisticat, getting down to work on a rustic ranch. How does she keep her claws so sharp with all of that hard work? Years of modeling must have taught her a lot of beauty secrets. All I can say is that she's more beautiful today than when she first appeared in those C'lawréal ads. Thanks for letting us readers have a peek behind the scenes of her real life. Purrhaps you could plan an upcoming story that examines her beauty secrets. I'd give anything to look like she does!

Marmalade
Atlanta, GA

Mewriah Carey

I have been a big fan of Mewriah Carey for some time. That kitty sure can howl! I enjoyed visiting with her, via the pages of your magazine, at her fabulous home in Beverly Hills. Now I can see why she is one of the queens of the music industry. She certainly lives like one on her palatial estate. All I can say is, "go, girl." Now that's what I call singing for your supper!

Snookems
Kenilworth, NJ

Send your letters to: Letters Editor, GOOD MOUSEKEEPING, NYC, NY. Only letters used in the column will be anspurred. Photos cannot be returned.

THE NEW GM GENERATION

Pansy & Sweet William Levy, ages 5 and 7 years

Goober Axelrod, 1 year old

David Axelrod

Tigger Parisi, 2 years old

Mickey Kats Zable, 7 years old

M. Maness

REIGNING CATS

Socks Clinton: Political Fat Cat

The sun streams over the South Lawn as the black and white tuxedo cat, wearing a red collar, surveys his domain. With only a leash to tether him to the property, Socks Clinton, the First Cat, reflects upon life in the public eye. There have been so many changes since he moved to Washington. The leash is perhaps the first constraint of celebrity. Back in the governor's mansion in Little Rock, Arkansas, such protective measures weren't necessary. He could roam the property freely and unafraid. But the glory of power must be tempered with caution. Political assassinations and kidnappings are now real considerations. The Secret Service has advised him that in order for them to assure his safety, he must submit to the indignity of a leash. Well, it's a small price to pay for fame.

The handsome cat presses his eyes closed for a moment, trying to focus clearly upon images from an earlier time. He remembers himself as a newborn kitten, only six years ago, abandoned by his mother at birth and placed in an adoptive home by a neighbor. Anita Reasoner, who was a piano teacher, took pity upon the helpless kitten and gave him to one of her students. The young girl was named Chelsea Clinton. Her father was the Governor of Arkansas, and before Socks knew it, he was caught up in the thrilling world of politics.

Life in the governor's mansion was always exciting. There were visitors to greet and special events to attend. Socks cut his teeth on the fast political pace and grew adept at socializing with a wide variety of people. These traits would serve him well when he made the leap to national politics and Washington.

The move to Washington was confusing. Socks had learned the ways of the local political machine and knew how to get his needs satisfied in an efficient manner. Now he would be starting from the ground up, learning the ropes and seducing a whole new support team with his feline charms. But he had survived by his wits before. He would take this new city, and the nation, by storm. He would make them his own.

The excitement of the Inauguration had barely subsided when Socks was called upon to host a Super Bowl party at The White House, where he entertained Governors Richards and Cuomo. In no time at all he had attracted the attention of the media, and only a month after he settled in, he was making his first television appearance on ABC News.

Socks has no official duties. He doesn't give interviews or make "purrsonal" appearances, but he feels that it is important to give something back to his loyal constituents, so he busies himself with his voluminous correspondence. He received one million pieces of mail in his first year in office, and he responds to every letter with an official photo card that bears the message, "Thank you for writing to me. I am honored to be your 'First cat.' Socks." Each note is "pawtographed" with his paw print.

Socks spends his days roaming around the White House. He occasionally greets visitors and enjoys playing on the South Lawn, which is closed to the public. Socks takes catnaps whenever he feels the urge, but his favorite place for cold weather napping is in one of the rooms where the heating equipment is kept. During the warm summer months he prefers to stretch out on one of the cool marble floors. He also enjoys perching in the many windows to look out at Washington and remain in touch with the plights of the common cat.

Socks eats dry cat food (the brand is not divulged for security purposes) and is cared for by members of the White House staff when the family is away. He does not choose to travel with the family on official visits, preferring the comforts of his luxurious home. And yes, he does use a litter box, which is located in the basement of the White House, in the engineers' office.

Socks is not the first feline to don the mantle of First Cat. George Washington had several cats, although they never resided in the White House. Abraham Lincoln was the first President on record

Q-T Cats Billy the Kid

NO BIZ LIKE SHOW BIZ

CFA Top Cats

Persian cats are the number one breed registered by the Cat Fanciers' Association, so it was little surprise when three Persians won the coveted titles of 1995 Best Cat of the Year, Best Kitten of the Year, and Best Cat in Premiership. The CFA is the world's largest registry of pedigreed cats. Founded in 1906, the CFA is a nonprofit organization of member clubs in the United States, Canada, and Japan, with international division member clubs in Argentina, Austria, Brazil, France, Germany,

Jadon Baskin-Robbins

Hong Kong, Italy, Monaco, the Netherlands, Russia, Singapore, Switzerland, Taiwan, and the United Kingdom. The organization sanctioned 426 shows in 1995 (366 in North America, 6 in Hawaii, 30 in Japan, and 24 in Europe), with total entries of 98,337 cats. The organization tallied point totals from all of these shows to arrive at the winners of their international awards.

Grand Champion, National Winner, Q-T Cats Billy the Kid, a red mackerel

tabby Persian male bred and owned by Marcia and Leon Samuels of Elkins Park, Pennsylvania, was named 1995 Best Cat of the Year.

The 1995 Best Kitten honors went to Grand Champion, National Winner, Chinois Come Back Little Diva, a black Persian female, bred and owned by Connie Chang of Los Angeles, California.

The third Persian to top the chart was named the Best Cat in Premiership. This classification is given to altered cats. Grand Champion, Grand Premier, National Winner Jadon Baskin-Robbins, a neutered cream Persian, was bred and owned by Donna and Susan Cook of Warrenton, Virginia. The eight-year-old male had the additional distinction of finishing the show season with a new record for premiership scoring, amassing 4,218.40 points.

When the points were added up for the last season, these three cats emerged victorious, each defeating the most cats in their respective classes. Our congratulations go to all of the winners, and we'll be looking for our readers at upcoming cat shows. For information on shows in your area, call the Friskies/CFA Cat Show Hotline, toll-free in the United States at 1(800) 725-4228.

to keep cats in the White House, and he was followed by Rutherford B. Hayes, Theodore Roosevelt, Woodrow Wilson, and Calvin Coolidge. Caroline Kennedy had a pet cat that resided for a short time in the White House. President Kennedy suffered from allergies, so the cat was sent to live with Jacqueline Kennedy's press secretary.

Socks has inspired the creation of a multitude of memorabilia and collectibles. Clothing, jewelry, mugs, bumper stickers, plush toys, and figurines are only a few of the many items that bear his likeness. There have even been two unauthorized biographies written for children: *When Socks Went to The White House*, by Harold Stearns; and *Socks Changes His Mind*, by Abell and Grubbs. These are only a few manifestations of our passion for the First Cat. We are proud of his fine and upstanding behavior and are encouraged by his efforts to present felines to the American public in such a favorable light.

Chinois Come Back Little Diva

LIKE CATS AND DOGS

The Dog Who Rescues Cats

A good number of our readers have never even met a dog, much less befriended one. Many of us subscribe to the old philosophy that cats and dogs are natural enemies. In the interest of dispelling this nasty rumor we present you with the story of Ginny, the dog who rescues cats.

The tale begins six years ago, in New York, where Ginny and her litter of newborn puppies were living in an apartment with a woman and her three children. The family was evicted from the apartment, and when the landlord went to check on what he thought was an empty apartment, he heard noises emanating from a locked closet. Upon opening the door, he was surprised to discover the small mixed-breed dog, emaciated, dehydrated, and carefully guarding her three puppies.

The four dogs were taken to a shelter and nursed back to health. Two of the puppies quickly found good homes, but the remaining puppy and the mother looked frail and required further nursing.

One day, a man and his female friend visited the shelter. The man had had a hard life. He had been involved in an industrial accident and had lost the use of his right arm and hand. He grew depressed and soon lost touch with his friends and family, preferring to bear his sorrows alone. A few months had passed, and he was falling deeper into despair. His one remaining friend grew concerned. She felt that he needed a reason to get up, get dressed, and go out every day. A dog could supply that reason. She convinced him to accompany her to the local animal shelter so that he could choose a dog.

Philip Gonzalez looked at every dog in the shelter. He thought that he wanted a macho dog, so when he found a Doberman in a cage, he felt his search was over. The Doberman was sharing her cage with another female dog, the scrawny dog we wrote about earlier. The shelter worker suggested that Philip

THE DOG WHO RESCUES CATS
THE TRUE STORY OF GINNY

PHILIP GONZALEZ AND LEONORE FLEISCHER
INTRODUCTION BY CLEVELAND AMORY

take the skinny, mixed-breed dog out instead. Just for a walk. Then he could decide. Against his better judgment, he agreed. The dog looked up at him and their eyes met. He thought that the small dog had "the most appealing face I'd ever seen, bright and intelligent, curious and sweet," so he decided to take the dog home. He named her Ginny.

One day when they were out for a walk together, Ginny began to pull him toward an abandoned lot. Philip let go of her leash and followed her. She approached a stray cat. Instead of chasing or attacking the cat, she began to lick and groom her, befriending her. Philip returned to the lot with food, and the hungry cat appeared with several friends. Ginny and Philip returned daily. Ginny had a special radar that attracted her to disabled cats who needed her care. She convinced Philip to take these cats home with them. Before long, they were sharing their apartment with fifteen handicapped cats, feeding and placing out countless others. Philip soon realized that this little dog had

CATALYST

Lend a Helping Paw: The Delta Society's Therapy Cats

The Delta Society is a nonprofit organization founded in 1977 to improve human health and well-being by promoting mutually beneficial contacts between people and animals. The organization has created a powerful network of pet owners, volunteers, healthcare employees, and scientists who believe a person or community is not healthy without nurturing contact with animals and nature. They are committed to educational and community service programs to make this belief a reality.

Special programs include an educational and referral center to expand understanding about how animals contribute to human health; helping pet owners deal with the death of an animal companion; training for health professionals in animal-assisted-therapy; advocating for the right of service dogs who assist people with disabilities to enter public places and the workplace; organizing national conferences; and operating the IAHAIO (headquarters for the International Association of Human-Animal Interaction Organizations) and Pet Partners.

Pet Partners may be of particular interest to our readers. It is a community service program through which cats, dogs, birds and other animals along with their human companions, visit nursing homes, hospitals, schools, treatment centers and other facilities. The pets share their time and love with people who need it most. We animals have a special, nonverbal way of communicating with people that can draw them out and soothe them. The Delta Society has established a specialized training program to teach us how to best interact with people, and they register graduates of the program so that their high standards are maintained.

Pets and their owners receive training in animal-assisted activities (AAA) or animal-assisted therapy (AAT). AAA

volunteers visit informally with hospital patients, nursing home residents, and people in other facilities. AAT volunteers work directly with therapists and become formally involved with patients' treatment regimens.

To become a Pet Partner, you must complete health, skills, and aptitude screening. You may receive training in a workshop or through a home study course. Upon paying a fee to the Delta Society, you will receive your registration packet, which contains information about an upcoming workshop in your area or the home study course, an ID card, and animal tag; details about insurance, newsletters, national awards, and networking; and offers for special shirts, capes, and vests.

Wanda, the cat pictured here, was rescued from the streets. She feels that it is her civic duty to give back some of the kindness that was extended to her during her time of need. She has therefore registered as a Pet Partner and visits hospitals and nursing homes to spread the love she was fortunate to receive. You, too, can share the magic of making a difference. Contact the Delta Society for a packet of materials about their many programs.

not only befriended him, she had given his life a new purpose. Perhaps, most astounding of all, he discovered that he loved cats and that Ginny loved them too.

Ginny is the subject of a book called *The Dog Who Rescues Cats*, written by Philip Gonzalez and Leonore Fleischer and published by HarperCollins. Look for this book packed with stories about Ginny and her feline friends.

CAT HOUSE

Pussies Galore at the Tree House Animal Foundation

The Tree House Animal Foundation was opened in 1971 by a group of Chicago humanitarians. Their objective was to provide healthcare and shelter for cats who might otherwise be euthanized. The shelter is located in an old Victorian house, and unlike other shelters, all cats roam free. No animals are confined to cages, and no cats are put to sleep unless they are in pain and terminally ill.

The foundation houses nearly three hundred cats at a time. Most are strays awaiting adoption, which the organization pursues aggressively through ads placed in local newspapers and magazines. Those cats that are difficult to place because of age or infirmity can live out their days at the shelter. The nonprofit organization relies upon donations for its support, and many people participate in a foster parent program, giving donations for the care of an animal who resides at the shelter.

The foundation is involved in a full range of community outreach programs

PAWTRAITS

The Puss in Pawtraiture

Cats are remarkably beautiful creatures. Don't ask us. Ask the countless artists who have captured our elusive images in a variety of media. People, in particular, seem to take great pleasure in the artistic representation of felines. Many of them have virtually dedicated their lives to immortalizing us in flat image and form.

Mimi Vang Olsen is renowned for her pet pawtraiture. She works from photographs she takes herself, so that

Mimi Vang Olsen

she spends time with each animal she paints, observing them to discern the small details that their human companions will recognize in their pawtraits. Her work can be seen on this page and in the illustrations we have included with our book excerpt from *The Breeders of Madison County*. Her work is also seen on the greeting cards and tee shirts sold for the benefit of the New York Humane Society.

Ponder Goembel is an illustrator known for her work in magazines and

Ponder Goembel

children's books. Her art is fanciful and dreamlike, evocative of fairy tales. She creates custom pawtraits of favorite felines working from photographs which she will return with the finished painting or drawing.

Priscilla Snyder creates vividly detailed sculptures of pets and their people from fabric and thread. She has devised a unique way of "painting" the fabric with sewing machine stitches

Priscilla Snyder

using a variety of colored threads. She has used as much as ten miles of thread in a single work. The fabric is stitched, stuffed, and assembled into a dramatic soft sculpture that achieves an amazing likeness to the subject. The finished work can be a head study or a full figure. The resulting sculpture can be displayed as art, or the piece can be designed to function as a jewel box, handbag, briefcase, suitcase, or puppet. Her work has been featured on TV and in magazines and newspapers, and it has appeared in galleries across the country. Because she works from photographs, a custom design can be commissioned from anywhere in the world.

Petography is the name of a pet photography studio run by Jim Dratfield and Paul Coughlin, who specialize in sepia-toned pawtraits of pets and their people. They also produce black-and-white pawtraits. They offer their photos matted in a frame of

Petography

your choice; on Victorian photo boxes; on custom-bound journals in leather, fabric, or wood; or on greeting cards. Their work has been featured in several books: *The Quotable Canine* (Doubleday), *The Quintessential Cat* (Prentice Hall), and *The Quotable Feline* (Knopf). They will travel to your home, or you can arrange to have your pet photographed at their studio in New York City.

that promote responsible pet care and ownership. Besides maintaining the adoption center, the group supports low-cost neuter, spay, and vaccination programs; a veterinary treatment center; animal rescue; cruelty investigations; an education program for school-age children; pet-facilitated therapy; newsletters and topical publications; radio, TV, and print public service announcements; services for low-income pet owners; the maintenance of a Pet Information

Hotline; and the support of a forty-acre environmental preserve.

The Pet Information Hotline is manned by trained Tree House counselors who provide sound, practical advice for pet-related problems. While the hotline is not a substitute for veterinary care, often a quick answer is what you need to steer you toward a solution. The hotline can be reached from 9 a.m. to 5 p.m. (Central time), seven days a week by dialing (312) 784-5488.

Petiquette for Today

BY SCRATCHING POST

This month I become the third generation of the Post family to be affiliated with Good Mousekeeping *as contributing predator of this column—and indeed it is an honor to be asked to continue in the tradition of my mistress and her mother-in-law.*

I look furward to getting to know you and giving careful thought to the questions in your letters. Thank you for reading my column. Maybe you'll learn something from it.

Unwelcome Gift

I am a gracious and thoughtful cat who believes in sharing my good fortune with others. I recently came upon a family of mice in the yard of my home. After eating my fill, there was still a mouse left over. I carried it into the house and left it on the kitchen counter as a surprise for my mistress (I know how much everyone likes surprises!). Then I went into the bedroom to take a nap. My sleep was disturbed by an eardrum-piercing scream! I awoke to find the poor woman running out the front door! We used to be the best of friends. Now she won't even look at me. What should I do?

People are strange animals. They are poorly brought up, lacking in manners, and do not accept gifts gracefully. Rather than descending to their level, be patient with them and elevate them to yours through education and example. Show them how to accept gifts graciously through your appreciative response when they bring you a treat or a toy. In time, you can resume giving your mistress gifts. Start out small. Begin with inanimate objects and work up to living things like mice and birds. If your person is even modestly intelligent, she should pick up on your example in no time at all. If she is as dense as I suspect they all are, give up. You deserve the mice more than she ever will!

Washed-up

I have noticed that my people bathe only once a day. Ugh! How do I teach them to maintain adequate hygienic standards, short of calling in the Department of Health?

You're right in your observation. Most people do bathe only once a day, and some bathe even less frequently! This may be attributed to the fact that people have a less finely developed sense of smell. If they could smell each other as well as we can, you could be sure that they'd pick up the schedule! In the meantime, there is little we can do to change their deplorable habits. I recommend that you just wash *yourself* wherever they touch you to prevent the spread of disease from their germ-ridden hands.

Unwanted Houseguest

I have always had a good relationship with the people who share my home. That is, up until recently. Without asking my permission, or even consulting with me, they have brought an intruder into my home. A large Labrador retriever puppy is sharing my bedroom. The beast is unruly and knows no manners. Why, he even eats from my bowl! The worst part is that I overheard one of the people saying that he isn't even fully grown! What nightmarish existence do I have before me?

You are right to be concerned. Labs are a particularly large breed of dog. What you see now is just a fraction of what you'll get in a year's time. If there is to be any sense of harmony in your home, you have to train that dog now to know who's boss. Aside from sheer size, you have several advantages over your housemate. First of all, you're a cat. You're a highly intelligent and refined creature, unlike dogs who are big and dumb. Cats are graceful and light on their feet, while dogs are sloppy and ungainly. Cats are clean; dogs are dirty. Cats use indoor plumbing; dogs must be walked in all kinds of weather. You get the idea... You can dance circles around the poor dog's head, and you should, if you must. Show him, and your people, how much easier and more fun it is to live with a cat. He'll learn who's boss and stay out of your way!

Kitty Bag

The woman that I live with dines out frequently. She often comes home with delectable little tidbits for me, which she has packed into a little bag at the restaurant. I never seemed to notice this before, but the bags are marked "Doggie Bag," and they bear an unattractive canine image on the front. Is it safe to eat the food from these bags?

Yes, it is safe, but it is unappetizing to dine from these sacks. These take-out bags were developed with gluttonous dogs in mind. Are you familiar with the term "chow hound"? Those animals have no finesse and will eat almost anything! I dislike the grotesque imagery that these bags engender. Ask your woman to request a plain, unmarked container at the restaurant. If this is not possible, have her discreetly transfer the food from the bag to your bowl before you enter the room, so as not to offend your sense of dignity.

On the Mark

Like most cats I know, I like to leave my mark on places, things and people who are important to me. I don't mean anything messy, like spraying, but simply rubbing my head against the leg of a chair or a person. It has come to my attention that my human companion has been wiping off my marks. Just today I found her rubbing the leg of one of my chairs with a soft piece of cloth. What is she doing? Is she rejecting my possessive gestures, or is she participating in some alien human rite?

There is no reason to be concerned. She is not rebuffing your advances; she is *re-buffing* the chair. Humans partake in a strange ritual called *dusting*. I'm sure you've seen it, although you may not have had a name for what they were doing. Dusting is a part of the activity they call cleaning. It runs contrary to our natural order. While we busy ourselves marking our space, people have an odd preoccupation with wiping things clean. We don't see where it does much good, as we will just re-mark the same items again and again, but it seems to make them feel good, so we let them do it.

YOU WAKE UP HAVING SLEPT THE SAME WAY
YOUR BED WAS CRAFTED. VERY WELL.

It is the revival of fine craftsmanship and timeless quality, finished in sturdy oak.
Its honest simplicity will last through years of cat naps. It is The American Shorthair Collection.
For more infurmation, call 1-800-CAT-NAPS. Ask for Dept. ZZZZ.

THE PLACE TO SLEEP IS *Tomcatville*

Your Questions Anspurred

BY JOYCE LITTERMATES, Ph.D.

New Baby at Home

My people have just brought home a new baby. They had the nerve to change everything without consulting me. The baby is living in my favorite room. The room is suddenly off-limits to me. They are especially upset when I hop into the baby's crib to get a look at her up close. I feel like they don't love me anymore. I was their favorite, and now all of the attention is going to her. How can I regain their attention and win back the affection that I've lost?

People have a strange attachment to their young. Unlike cats who sever the parental bond when our kittens are young, humans retain a strong tie with their offspring forever. Even though you may have been their favorite, all that has now changed. You'll have to develop new and acceptable modes of behavior to adjust to your changed role.

Don't harbor resentment against the new baby. To antagonize the baby will only further alienate your people's affection toward you. It is better if you develop a system of coping with the new familial structure, which will set your people at ease, and reassure them that you love them, and the baby, still.

Approach the baby slowly and cautiously. Avoid touching or licking the baby. Humans have a funny fear of what they call germs; they do not realize that you are simply trying to keep their offspring clean. Do not make loud noises near the baby, which may cause her to cry.

Focus your attention on the adults, instead. Do not be aggressive in your attempts to gain their concern. A little interaction will go a long way during this stressful period of readjustment.

Your people still love you, and as soon as they have had their fill of crying, diapers, and late-night feedings, they'll remember who they love best!

Boyfriend Blues

The woman I live with is single, and I have always been the love of her life. Suddenly a man has come into the picture, and I don't like it a bit. He is intruding upon my home, and he acts as if he owns the place. It took me years to settle into the cushion just so, and he's messing up all my hard work. I have to laugh when he gets up, however, because his pants are covered in my long, white hair. He doesn't find this funny and sometimes swats at me with the newspaper when my lady isn't looking. She thinks he's wonderful and doesn't see his many faults. I'm afraid that one day he'll move in and take over. What can I do?

Men can be a problem. We spend years training a woman to cater to our every whim, and overnight, it seems, she forgets everything we taught her. Women are easy to manipulate, as you have undoubtedly discovered over the years of living with yours. You must take the upper hand and not let some big oaf take over what is rightfully yours.

The best way to regain your woman's love, and to infuriate the big jerk, is to be extra affectionate to **both** of them. Why, you might ask? If you are extra attentive to her, she'll eat it up. Men can't be nearly as soft and cuddly as we are. Women are so used to chasing after us for our attention, that your mistress will be overwhelmed at her good fortune and will remember how very much she loves you in the first place.

If you kill him with kindness, he'll be so repulsed by all the attention from you that he'll alienate you in any way he can, and that's just what you want. If he is mean or nasty to you, just make sure that your woman sees it. She'll recognize that he is just like all men, a rude brute who is unkind to soft and helpless creatures like yourself. She'll realize that a man like him has no place in your home, and before you know it, he'll be history.

If he's clever enough to see through your manipulations, as few are, he'll learn to stay out of your way, or ignore you. So in both cases, you'll get to do exactly what you want, and live as you did before.

Feline Artistry

I am a sensitive cat with a fine aesthetic appreciation for beauty. I take great pleasure in creating works of art in my home. Only this morning I tipped over a houseplant and spread the soil on the floor in great concentric circles. It was a powerful piece, and I named it *Earth Spheres*. Following that, I used my claws to create a feathery effect on the arm of a chair. I call this work *Bird in Flight*, after Brancusi. My people, who obviously have not attended a program in art appreciation, fail to see the beauty or recognize the genius in my works. They grow very upset each time they see one of my masterpieces. How can I enlighten them to the complexity of my art?

You're right. People are often unsophisticated beings. It's little wonder that the word *sophisticate* contains the word cat. But so much for my observation. You are seeking a solution, and a solution you will receive. People have tremendous difficulty recognizing great art when they see it. If you think you are having trouble with them at home, you can't begin to imagine the human comments that have been overheard in museums! So you are truly not alone. This is a common problem, with emphasis upon the term *common*. People have not been exposed to the advantages that we have. They have not grown up around art and beautiful things, as we have. So they are ignorant and fail to recognize beauty when they see it.

Do not hold this shortcoming against your people. They cannot help their limitations. It's who they are. Be tolerant. You might try to curtail your artistic activity for a while. It is difficult to enjoy producing art without an appreciative audience. If you must persist in your artistic pursuits, try working on a smaller scale. A small thread drawn discretely from beneath the bed or sofa makes an equally appealing medium, and you won't suffer the unfortunate consequences of their ignorance.

Katex introduces guaranteed protection.

The piddlepant guaranteed to work purrfectly when your self-control doesn't.

Katex understands that there are times when you can't go outside or reach a litter box. Perhaps you just don't want to. You have your reasons. The Katex Purrsonals Protective Piddlepants fit you purrfectly, and they're completely disposable. But best of all, they let you do your own thing and still maintain a relationship with your people. So you feel more safe and secure, even on your most ornery days. We guarantee it.* Try Katex Purrsonals. Your people will thank you for it.

Katex understands.

The Helclawise Helpline

Dangerous Decorations

Dear Helclawise: I enjoy the festive look of my home around holiday time each year. I can't help but wonder, however, if some of the decorative items might pose a danger to me and other cats. I am purrticularly concerned about strings of lights, which can be deadly if chewed, as well as seasonal plants like poinsettias. What special tips can you offer to cats who live in homes that feature these holiday displays?

—*Katmandu*

You are right to bring up these potential problems for cats and other pets. Tell your people to avoid bringing plants like poinsettias into the house. We all know what a tasty temptation these plants present, but they can be poisonous if eaten. Stay away from the holiday lights. Besides risking electrocution if you chew on them, you can become seriously tangled in their cords if you play with them unattended. Stick to something safer, like yarn or string, if you wish to become hopelessly entangled in something fun. Stay away from wrapping paper and ribbons. As tempting as these things might be, they contain dangerous chemicals and dyes, and swallowing them can make you sick. That goes for holiday treats, as well. These treats are prepared by humans for human consumption. They contain substances that can be dangerous or deadly to cats. And they're fattening besides. So leave the junk food to people. Stay healthy by eating your regular diet at holiday time, as well as the rest of the year.

Reknitting Sweaters

Dear Helclawise: How do you reknit a sweater after you have unraveled it? My female human companion has a favorite sweater that she treasures dearly. I have improved its design with the addition of several attractive large holes across the front. I thought that they would provide much needed-ventilation since the yarn is heavy and the sweater must be too warm. I also took the liberty of unraveling the cuffs and shortening the sleeves, so that her wrists would be exposed to the cool air. Besides, it was tasty, and I had fun doing it. Anyway, I left the sweater out on the bed for her to see. You can imagine my surprise when she hit the roof and screamed at me for an hour! Then she burst into tears, and she hasn't spoken to me since. How can I restore the sweater to its former condition?

—*Coco*

I'm afraid that there's no easy answer to your question. Learning to knit is a complex skill, which requires more time and space to explain than I can devote in this column. I recommend that your person discard the sweater. I'm sure that it will be impossible to repair, and she will feel bad every time she sees it.

People have an odd fashion sense. I'm certain that she did not see the beauty and practicality of your alterations. Try to refrain from redesigning her clothes in the future. Save your aesthetic sense for things more deserving of your time and talents, like big, permanent pieces of furniture, sofas and chairs, that she will be less likely to discard as easily.

Hair Remover

Dear Helclawise: I am a dark-colored cat who lives with my people in a light-colored home. I have no problem with this arrangement, but they are always complaining about the dark hair that they find on every surface. I think that these dark hairs are a colorful addition to their bland decor, but they do not share my enlightened opinion. How can we resolve this disagreement?

—*Blackie*

I would recommend that they redecorate their home in a color complementary to your fur. Black is a good choice for most rooms in the house. This would be the simplest way to make your hair blend with the decor. If they are unwilling to try this easy solution, they will just have to remove the loose, offending hairs in a conventional manner. Following you from room to room with an adhesive lint roller is one way to alleviate the contrasting hairs. Vacuum cleaners, special squeegees, and spongelike fur magnets are other devices that might be helpful. I wish your people good luck in this hopeless quest. You might also try to purrsuade them to appreciate your contrasting hairs as a clever decorative accent. This has worked well in some feline homes.

A Growing Concern

Dear Helclawise: I enjoy plant life as much as the next cat. My people were kind enough to install a collection of attractive, and tasty, plants on the windowsills of my home. I liked snacking on these plants and occasionally used the soil instead of my litterbox. I'm not certain if they've discovered my secret habits, but I have suddenly found my favorite haunts off-limits. They've put sticky tape on all of the window sills and removed all the dead and damaged plants. How can I restore the status quo?

—*Snowflake*

I'm not sure how they found out what you were up to, but they did. They've obviously installed these barriers to keep you away from the plants, and it seems to be working. The best way to have them restore the former balance is to create a compelling reason for them to recreate the outdoors inside. By this I mean try to slip out of the house any chance you get. If you make this quick-escape routine a habit, they'll try to think of ways to keep you indoors. If they're smart (and you're lucky), they'll bring back the plants as a way of simulating the outdoor experience within. I wish you the best of luck in purrsuading your people to bring back your indoor garden.

A Powerful New World of Cat Hair Removal

Now there's Eurekat. The vacuum which makes your house and furnishings fur-free. No more unsightly drop cloths, foolish lint rollers, or evil electronic devices designed to keep you off your favorite chair.

Special features include:
- Lots of tools to get hair out of all the nooks and crannies of your home.

- Hose is permanantly attached, to be ready to go anytime, day or night.

- Eurekat's unique filtration system keeps loose hair in the vacuum bag—not in the machinery where it can stuff up the works.

Eurekat helping our world.
The Eurekat Company will donate a portion of the purrchase price of each vacuum sold to a research foundation which is seeking to combat hair loss in cats.

Call 1-800-FUR-FLYS for the name of your local Eurekat dealer.

World Class Hair-Removal From The People Who Care About Your World

EUREKAT
VACUUM HAIR REMOVAL DEVICES

CATSUMERS' GUIDE

Litter Boxes

Scratch 'n' sniff. Finally, litter boxes that really work. The newest designs consider what we actually do in there and are engineered for convenience and hygiene. Here, our 7 favorites.

The litter box has become standard in feline households. In the past a cat had to resort to "outdoor plumbing." After a time, indoor provisions were made for the family house cat. The first litter boxes were simple pan affairs, not unlike the common baking dish, filled with sand or sawdust, to simulate the soil we encountered during our forays into the wild. As cats grew in popularity to the highly regarded animals we are today, the technologies associated with feline waste removal improved in equal proportion. Highly absorbent cat box fillers gave way to odor control formulas, and today litters that clump when they receive liquid waste are growing in popularity.

Today's cat craves convenience without compromising cleanliness. The new litter formulas make this combination easy to achieve. Clumping litters make it simple and almost pleasant for our people to scoop out our boxes often, if not daily. The most innovative litter box designs combine privacy with ease of use (both for us, and for those who clean up the mess). Some are actually "self-cleaning." Well, almost. The person has to help.

How We Chose

We put the boxes to actual use with a variety of cats. Okay, they were our friends. But they were a discriminating bunch. As all of us are. Some boxes had better features than others. Some were no-nonsense and purrformed the job as expected. A few had all the bells and whistles. But when all is said and done, each one did the job. And so did we.

BOODALOO

**Boodaloo from Aspen Pet Products
Phone: (303) 375-1001**
Features: Flap-door, covered box. Maximum privacy. Deodorizing panels. Basic design in Booda line.
Comments: Private and easy to use. The flap door can take some getting used to. Most difficult top to remove for cleaning.

BOODABOX

**Boodabox from Aspen Pet Products
Phone: (303) 375-1001**
Features: The standard Booda design, which was revolutionary when it was first developed. The top clasps shut. Lots of interior room. Deep capacity. Deodorizing panels in lid. Clear windows to permit your people to spy on you under the guise of checking for cleanliness.
Comments: A fine utilitarian box. Lots of nice features. The snap-shut clasp makes this a bit difficult for your people to gain access for cleaning.

Use & Care Tips

1. Do we really have to tell you what to do? Where was your mother?

2. Okay, first step all the way into the box. Tail and everything.

3. Squat. Do what comes naturally.

4. Using your paws, cover up the evidence.

5. Hop out quickly, taking care not to scatter too much litter as you make your hasty retreat.

6. Lick yourself scrupulously clean.

7. Assume a nonchalant demeanor, ignoring any odors that may be emanating from the box.

BOODABOX HINGED LID

**Boodabox with hinged lid from Aspen Pet Products
Phone: (303) 375-1001**
Features: The most advanced Boodabox design. Enhanced Boodabox with the added convenience of a hinged lid that flips up for easy cleaning.
Comments: The best design in this line. All the features of the original with the bonus of a flip-top lid.

BOODA ZERO-MAX

Booda Zero-Max from Aspen Pet Products
Phone: (303) 375-1001
Features: The most innovative design from Boodabox. The box is ergonomically designed to permit easy entrance through a broad covered door. The space-age lines work well with most decors. The top retracts into itself at the touch of a button, permitting this design to fit into the tightest spaces.
Comments: The box appears to be an improvement over the earlier Booda designs. We were supplied with an early sample, so we did not have the opportunity to put it through its paces, but the mechanism appeared to work smoothly. We look forward to giving this box a try. It's good-looking and fun to use.

DRY SYSTEM

The Dry System from Sweet P
Phone: (716) 285-9000
Features: A unique drainage system permits the rapid absorption and elimination of liquid wastes. Solid wastes remain on the surface, awaiting manual disposal by your human.
Comments: The idea is sound, but the actualization is a bit unattractive between clean-ups. A planned cover, shaped like a fancy building or gazebo is a good idea.

KITTEN CABOODLE

Kitten Caboodle from Omega Paw
Phone: (800) 222-8269
Features: This box is self-cleaning through the use of clumping litter. The box rolls over and the used litter is sifted through a filtering grill, which collects the solid clumps of waste. The waste is contained in a pull-out tray which can be easily disposed of in a hygienic manner.
Comments: The most innovative design we tested, and it seems to work. We tested an earlier generation of the design, so the operation should be improved by the time the actual product reaches the shelves of a store near you.

THE ELIMINATOR

The Eliminator from Pet Products Warehouse
Phone: (800) 575-4593
Features: A unique, new design. Box is aerated so that liquid wastes evaporate before bacteria can form to produce unpleasant odors.
Comments: Time constraints prevented a test run, but the box appears to be well designed, and the idea behind the design seems sound.

Features to Look For

✔**Covered boxes:** These afford you the greatest degree of privacy. Some boxes have flap doors or deeply sloping entrances, which are particularly dog-resistant.

✔**Hinged lids:** Tops swing open effortlessly making it easier for your people to gain access when they clean up.

✔**Deodorizing panels:** Special materials are incorporated into the design that absorb and neutralize foul odors.

✔**Deep capacity:** Litter boxes that accommodate a large quantity of litter. Good for active cats, large cats, or multiple-cat homes.

✔**Litter-trapping mats:** Grooved panels at the entrance to the litter box trap and collect loose litter that adheres to your feet. This prevents the litter from scattering on the floor.

✔**Drainage systems:** Some of the new boxes work on a unique principle of neutralizing odor through evaporation.

✔**Self-cleaning designs:** Some of the new boxes incorporate a roll-over design, where the used litter is sifted through a screen that traps the wastes and collects them in a box, which can be easily removed and emptied. These are the closest thing to "self-cleaning" to date. But, hey, what do we really care? We don't have to do the dirty work!

Shop Smart

✔ **What do you really need?** Consider the features that are most important to you. Do you crave the privacy of a covered box? Is paying a premium price for a self-cleaning box necessary?

✔**Compare price.** Many of these boxes are available from a large variety of sources, from local pet shops to superstores, from warehouse markets to mail-order catalogs. Explore the pricing options completely.

✔ **Finally, ask your people which design they prefer.** After all, they are the ones who will be doing all the cleaning, and if it isn't convenient for them, you will be the one who ultimately suffers most.

Introducing Nine Lives
for your Floors.

Mr. Claw just discovered the way to keep the kittenish glow on your shiny new floor. That's something you can't count on from your old floor cleaner. Over time, it will leave a waxy build-up that shows every paw print. Even licking your floor clean without a cleanser will leave your floor streaky with tongue marks. But Mr. Claw for Neater Floors lifts and removes dirt safely, and deliciously. Its delightful mouse flavor makes licking your floors clean a treat. So as time goes on your floor will keep on looking great. (Through all its nine lives.)

Mr. Claw tastes best!

Crocheted Catnip Mice

An easy, inexpensive way to turn yarn into pretty treasures

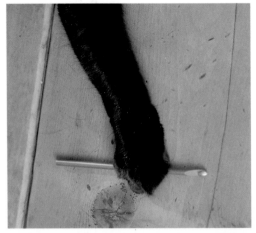

❶ Mice, mice, mice. What do we like better than mice? And when they are combined with the scent of catnip and the texture of yarn, we can't think of a more delectable treat. Turn your time in the workbasket into something productive. Just follow these easy instructions to stitch up your own family of mice in an assortment of realistic colors.

❷ Materials. A wicker workbasket filled with balls of yarn in an assortment of colors—grays and white; a length of pink yarn for the eyes; a crochet hook, in a size that is easy to grasp in your paw (we like G, H, or I); a small pair of scissors to trim excess yarn; a tapestry needle; dried catnip, a teaspoonful for each mouse; and fiberfill to stuff finished mice.

❸ Head, body, and tail. Holding the crochet hook in your front right paw, complete **RND 1** by ch 2, 4 sc in 2nd ch from hook. Don't join together.--4 sts. **RND 2** (Sc in next st, 2 sc in next st) twice--6 sts. **RND 3** (Sc in next 2 sts, 2 sc in next st) twice--8 sts. **RND 4** (sc in next 3 sts, 2 sc in next st) twice--10 sts. **RND 5** (2 Sc in next st, sc in next st) three times, sc in next 4 sts--13 sts. **RND 6** Sc in each st around. **RND 7** (Sc next 2 sts tog, sc in next 4 sts) twice, sc in next st--11 sts. **RND 8** Sc in each st around. **RND 9** 2 Sc in next st, sc in next st, 2 sc in each of next 2 sts, sc in next st, 2 sc in next st, sc in next 5 sts--15 sts. **RND 10** Sc in each st around. **RND 11** Sc in next 3 sts, (2 sc in next st, sc in next st) four times, sc in next 4 sts--19 sts. **RNDS 12-14** Sc in each st around. *(continued)*

Catnip Mice, cont'd

RND 15 Sc in next 3 sts, (sc next 2 sts tog, sc in next st) five times, sc in nest st--14 sts. **RND 16** Sc in each st around. **RND 17** Sc in next 4 sts, (sc next 2 sts tog) four times, sc in next 2 sts--10 sts. Stuff, adding catnip in center of fiberfill. **RND 18** Sc in next 2 sts, (sc next 2 sts tog) four times--6 sts. **RND 19** (Sc next 2 sts tog) twice, make one sl st through front lps of next 2 sts, chain 10, sl st in next 8 sts, sl st in same front lps of last rnd. Fasten off.

❹ **Ears.** **ROW 1** Ch 2, 3 sc in 2nd ch from hook, ch 1, turn. **ROW 2** Sc in first sc, 3 sc in next sc, sc in last sc. Fasten off. Cup slightly and sew ears to Rnds 5 and 6 of head.

Finishing. Using pink yarn, embroider two eyes on face.

If all this seems confusing or too difficult, put down the crochet hook and tapestry needle. Go to the wicker workbasket filled with multicolored balls of yarn. Play with yarn balls (after all, they're as much fun as the crocheted mice, and much less work. And who ever said that work is fun?) Enjoy!

Crocheted Catnip Mice Pattern courtesy of the book, Boutique Bonanza, *published by KC Publishing, Inc.* Boutique Bonanza *can be purchased by sending $9.95 plus $2.50 shipping and handling to KC Publishing, Inc., Department GM, 700 West 47th Street, Suite 310, Kansas City, MO 64112 or by using a major credit card and calling 1-800-878-7855.*

**Before my free
Mewle Norman makeover.**

My nose was too pink.

I groomed constantly.

I licked my whole body clean.

I always looked tired.

I felt fat.

I ran from the slicker brush.

I felt uncomfortable wearing a collar.

**After my free
Mewle Norman makeover.**

My nose is still pink.

I still do.

I use my paw to wash my face.

I take more naps.

Fat is beautiful.

Brushing keeps my fur fluffy.

I still feel uncomfortable wearing a collar.

*A trained Mewle Norman Beauty Advisor can help you to learn to like the fur you were born with —
in a relaxed, no-pressure atmosphere. Whether you want simple grooming tips,
a color analysis, a fur-care lesson or a complete makeover, it's free.
So come in now and learn how to love what you've got.*

*For the Studio nearest you or to discover the beauty of running a Mewle
Norman Catsmetics Studio, call 1-800-FUR-FACE.*

MEWLE NORMAN®
CATSMETIC STUDIOS
The Place for the Furry Face.™

New Irish Cream.
Escape to your own Creamy World.

BEAUTY MEWS

- **Name:** Catsandra Furface
- **Age:** 5
- **Occupation:** House cat and resident mouser, Queens, NY.
- **Family:** She has 12 kittens, none living at home.
- **Beauty problem:** "I have fly away fur. Static makes my coat look unruly. Grooming gives me furballs. And I seem to leave a trail of hair behind me wherever I go. What can I do to achieve a more polished appearance?"

MAKEOVER OF THE MONTH

To create head-turning hair we used the "less is more" approach—frequent brushing to remove old, dead hair. It's better to find excess hair in your brush than on everyone and everything in sight. Daily brushing removes the hair that you shed constantly, and your coat will look glossy and clean from the regular attention. **Tools of the trade:** Use a wire slicker brush, Purebred pet mitt, or ZoomGroom to stimulate circulation and remove loose fur. **If your shedding is particularly severe (or if the people you live with are allergic),** you may have to submit to dreaded baths. (Ugh!) Sometimes a simple water rinse may be sufficient to remove loose hair and cat dander, but a real bath—in a tub, with shampoo—may be the only solution to your problem. While this may appear to be a catastrophic measure and more horrific than the problem itself, we can assure you that, in time, the fear and shock of soap and water to your system will subside, and you may even take pleasure in this alien ritual. **Products to reduce shedding:** Shedaway (available at your local pet store) and Loshed (available through your veterinarian) are products designed to reduce nonessential shedding. The topically applied preparations can reduce shedding by over 50% in 8 out of 10 cats. Try one of these products if your loose hair is making you an unwelcome member of your family. **Last resort:** If none of these measures seem to work, we recommend the manual approach of hair removal, after the fact. Adhesive pet hair rollers, 3M's Pat-it pet hair remover, Gonzo pet hair lifter, and Furniture Magnet are only a few of the ways to clean up loose hair from surfaces throughout your home. It even works on your people!

Kiss and Makeup: Feline Beauty Accessories

It was only a matter of time before people began to design beauty products in our feline image. Major cosmetic companies are using cats to sell their beauty products to feline-obsessed women. We always knew that they were crazy about us, we just didn't realize that their admiration for our lithe appearance would lead to compacts and other beauty accessories that bear our likeness.

Estée Lauder
The cosmetic giant has embraced the small cat in an assortment of compact designs. While the specific designs are subject to change from year to year, current offerings include the Cat Nap compact for pressed powder—shown here—and the Cat's Meow, which contains solid purrfume in the Pleasures fragrance. You can find these at your local Estée Lauder counter, with additional offerings during the holiday season.

Debbie J. Palmer
This new company specializes in beautiful purse accessories. The Contented Cats collection was inspired by Ms. Palmer's cat, Mozart, pictured here. Mozart's favorite napping place is in a large

Chinese bowl. His naptime appearance is similar to that of the circular cat seen in the compact for pressed powder. A fragrance flacon, pill box, mirror, picture frame, and candle holder complete the feline collection. When he is not working hard, sleeping to inspire his mistress, Mozart can be found in the recording studio. The multitalented cat is the vocalist you hear in the famous Meow-Mix commercials.

BEAUTY MEWS

CLAW COVERS
Do They Really Work?

Cats have a natural tendency to exercise their claws. We enjoy sharpening our nails on a variety of surfaces, from the smooth woods of furniture and the soft fabrics of curtains, to the firmer and sometimes nubby textures of upholstery. As much as we love our exercise and the result-

ing "artwork," our human companions look upon our handiwork in horror. Where we see "artistry," they see "damage." There is no way to educate these dim-witted humans into a full appreciation of our talents, so we must seek ways to effect a compromise. How can we exercise our paws without incurring the wrath of our people? Or without losing our claws? **Our Recommendation:** A veterinarian has developed a painless system of claw covers which attach to our claws by means of a harmless adhesive. Soft Paws can be applied by a veterinarian, or, if they are particularly adept, by your people. The soft plastic covers must be replaced every 4 to 6 weeks, but they are a small compromise when compared to the alternative! **The Results:** We found the Soft Paws to be a useful product. While they did eliminate our ability to leave our mark around the house, this drawback was offset by the beauty benefits Soft Paws provide. The covers come in a variety of attractive, bright colors, which look remarkably like nail polish. Just think of Soft Paws as artificial nails for cats. There's nothing like a touch of color to perk up your appearance. We rate Soft Paws two paws up!

The Fur's Flying

Sometimes it is difficult for us to share our homes with people. They have such silly notions about cleanliness. We are scrupulously clean creatures, purrhaps even more vigilant about purrsonal hygiene than they are. Humans bathe only once a day, while we groom constantly. It is therefore ironic that they take such displeasure in a natural by-product of our grooming—loose hair. We purrceive this fine scattering of hair as a gift—more of us to love. Humans appear annoyed, no, disgusted by the fur we leave behind on every surface. While we may never reconcile our difference of opinion, in the interest of harmony GM recommends several products to reduce the loose hair in your home. **Immunovet** manufactures two lines of products to reduce shedding, **Shedaway** and **Loshed. ZoomGroom** and the **Purebred** pet mitt are two other ways to fight loose hair at its source. If these methods do not sufficiently reduce the amount of hair in your home, you may wish to try surface hair removers. The **Gonzo** pet hair lifter, the **Furniture Magnet,** and **3M's Pat-it** are three new methods to use. If all else fails, you can use an adhesive pet hair roller or tape to pick up any remaining stray hairs.

Paws for Reflection

Every puss deserves a little pampering. We have to train our people to indulge us in every way. While they are generous with our feeding, grooming, and other physical requirements, they often fail to focus on our psychic needs. Cats are spiritual creatures. We have a finely tuned sixth sense and require time to get in touch with our New Age values. We must therefore acquaint our people with relaxation therapies to promote our sense of wellness.

One time-honored technique is to achieve a sense of serenity through massage. The book *How to Massage Your Cat,* by Alice M. Brock (of "Alice's Restaurant" fame), promotes well-being through a healing touch. A more hands-off approach to serenity can be achieved by listening to the self-help tape *Finding Your Inner Purr: The Cat Lover's Guide To Relaxation.* Or just find a cozy spot and curl up for a nap...

HOW TO MASSAGE YOUR CAT

ALICE M. BROCK

Purrfection

The first-ever collector plate
in fine pawcelain from the popular
magazine **Good Mousekeeping**.

What could be more finicky than Morris the Cat? So discriminating —so irrepressible—and ready to capture your heart! This is the subject of "Purrfection." An endearing pawtrait of your favorite *Good Mousekeeping* cover cat—on a very limited edition collector plate from The Furanklin Mint, whose works are prized by knowledgeable cat collectors throughout the world.

In the tradition of only the finest collectibles, this heirloom plate is paw-crafted of the finest pawcelain, and Morris is painted with such painstaking detail that he seems to breathe as he looks back at you. The plate is paw-numbered, and bears the *Good Mousekeeping* seal of approval to assure you of its fine quality.

This plate has been crafted in an *extremely* limited edition, it is truly one-of-a-kind, and as such, it is priceless and unavailable for sale to our readers. You may write to us, using the printed coupon, to beg us to part with our irreplaceable plate, but we assure you that it is unique, ours alone, and you cannot have it.

Cindy Clawfurd

Glamour Puss

You don't have to be born beautiful to look this gorgeous, but it sure helps. These fabulous felines have worked hard to achieve the look of effortless beauty. But even a plain puss can be transfurmed into something special if you take their advice.

Naomi Catbell

Naomi Catbell

"I was a humble street cat in London, but I always had big dreams. I knew that I had good bones, I was long and slender. And I had a beautiful dark coat. So I started out more fortunate than most. It took hard work to become the supurrmodel I am today. I fight against a cat's natural tendency to curl up into a ball and nap all day. And I watch what I eat. While I really like red meat (especially mice), I try to stick to a spartan but balanced diet of dry food. Great clothes help, like this spectacular 'Calvin Claw' creation from Razz Pe' Tazz."

Cindy Clawfurd

"I grew up in a regular litter. I had no idea that I'd end up where I am today, a supurrmodel, spokescat, and actress. I have worked under exclusive contract for Rexlon and was married to a Hollywood star. But throughout it all, I worked hardest at becoming an astute business purrson. How do I maintain my good looks? Heredity helps. The rest has to come from you. Sure, I could lay around all day and scarf down cat treats. Yet I fight against the feline inclination to rest and instead work out with my purrsonal trainer. Clothes make the cat. My leopard-spotted ultrasuede bandanna is from UltraMouse. There's nothing like spots to lift a cat's spirits!"

Clawdia Schiffur

Clawdia Schiffur

"I'm originally from Germany. I was discovered in my homeland and made the trip to America. I was a tall and gawky kitten. No one who knew me then could have predicted that I would be celebrated as a great beauty today. My beauty secrets are not so secret. We all know what we have to do. It's just that not every cat is interested in eating and living correctly. My German sense of discipline is helpful in enforcing that I eat the right things (canned food is my favorite, and I prefur fish), exercise (like most supurrmodels, I have made my own videotape), and get enough sleep (that's the easy part!). I became the best I could be, I wear great clothes (like this gold, bejeweled 'Chatnel' collar from Tanner & Dash), and I met my Prince Charming (David Coppurrfield). 'Poof.' Just like magic, I have it all!"

Uma Purrman

"I'm known for my unusual beauty. My bedroom eyes may be my best feature. I

Uma Purrman

attribute them to the long naps I take every day. Because I spend so much time in bed, I have little time left to eat. That's how I watch my diet. Acting is hard work. You come in for an early call and often sit around all day waiting to be called to the set. I require a comfurtable trailer, so I can get plenty of sleep. It's probably my best beauty advice. I also get a lift from wearing beautiful clothes, like this diamanté pavé collar from Allison Craig Rare Petware."

Demi Meower

Demi Meower

"Who would believe that I would go from being one of the young 'Rat Pack' actors to the highest paid actress in Hollywood? Certainly not I! It takes hard work to balance a family (I'm married to actor Burmese Willis and have young kittens) with the demands of a career. My latest movies have required nude scenes. To most cats this is no great trick, since we're naked most of the time anyway. But how many of you appear in close-up on the big screen, enduring the scrutiny of the whole world? Not many, I might imagine. So I have to look my best at all times, but especially on-screen. I work out with a purrsonal trainer, and carefully monitor my diet, which is rich in fish, because like most cats, I dislike vegetables. I look after my fur, because in a way, it looks after me. I like minimally-designed clothes the best. Like this collar from Tanner & Dash."

Linda Evanpurrlista

"I am the chameleon of the modeling industry. I like to experiment with lots of different looks. You never know what color my fur will be next. Nor do I! I'm naturally thin, and my looks are not conventionally beautiful, but I am always striking, dramatic, and truly original. You can't look like me because I can't look like me! I'm never the same cat twice. I am the

Linda Evanpurrlista

spokescat for Clawrol Furcolor, and with good reason. I enjoy wearing beautiful clothes like this 'Chatnel' Ultrasuede and chain collar and leash from UltraMouse."

Nicole Kitten

"I was born and raised in Australia and came to America to act. I met my husband, actor Tomcat Cruise, on the set of a film. Today I balance my life between family (we have two kittens) and career. I am finally being considered for challenging film roles. I maintain my good looks through a stressful but fulfilling schedule. I have little time or opportunity to eat the wrong things. I must set a good example for my kittens if they are to develop healthy eating habits. I prefur to eat natural, raw things, like sushi and mice. An occasional bird is good too. I get plenty of exercise and lots of sleep. I like to spend my free time doing things for my family. I even made my collar myself, from a home sewing pattern by Simplicity." ★

Nicole Kitten

STYLE MEWS

How I Got My Style

Kattie Lee Gifurred, star of the popular TV show Outregis and Kattie Lee, *shares her fashion secrets.*

Age: Younger than you.

Life style: Happily married to Furank, with two kittens, Caty and Catsidy.

Bargain Basics: I purrchase all of my clothes at Wild-Mart, from the Kattie Lee Collection, which I design myself. No kitten labor is ever used in the manufacture of my products. The line is comfurtable, attractive, and, most of all, affurdable.

Pet Project: I am the spokescat for Carnivore Cruise Lines and appear in all their commercials. You know the ones, "Carnivore's got the fur...." It is a demanding role, and I have to wear all kinds of form-fitting costumes. My favorites are the catsuits.

Catanetics: I am currently at work on an exercise video. It's called "Mommycise." The focus of the program, like everything else in life, is your kittens. You can't imagine how many calories you burn by carrying your kittens around everywhere you go! Which reminds me of my newest project. I am developing a line of exercise equipment—which I use in the video—including a cat carrier designed to accommodate a full litter of kittens. The larger your brood, the greater the health benefits!

Mouse & Garden: I look furward to my private time, which I

Kattie Lee Gifurred, Chaircat of Fashion.

spend at home with my family. Unfortunately, my schedule has been so full that I have not had much time to get back home to Connecticat. So I do the next best thing. I bring my family with me wherever I go—to the TV studio, to Wild-Mart, and even on the Carnivore cruises! I know that my fans want to be just like me. It's just a matter of setting your priorities, sticking to your goals, and always giving something back to those who are less furtunate.

Catsquerade!

We all like to dress up in something special for a party or holiday event. Cats enjoy wearing costumes, but up until recently, there were not many choices for discriminating felines. Two companies have come to the rescue. Flytes of Fancy produces a full line of costumes, including the devil suit you see here. They are colorful, comfortable, and really cute. Cats who possess sewing skills (or those who live with people who do) will be pleased to discover home sewing pattern number 9257 from Simplicity Crafts. It features a selection of eight costumes, including seasonal favorites like Santa Claws and a jack-o'-lantern. They're easy to make and fun to wear.

Catbird Seat

Break free of your confining carrier. Travel up front, with a view of the world! The Pet Pouch was designed with dogs in mind, but docile and well-behaved kitties will be rewarded with a snuggly experience. Imagine, the wind in your face and the full support of your loving person. We can't think of a better way to travel.

Sew Smart

Handy cats have lots of home-sewing options. Simplicity has produced a collection of craft patterns for cats (and those with people who sew). Pattern number 9065 features seven different bed designs. The pattern also includes a fish-shaped place mat for fine dining. A new pattern will soon be available for a group of pet carriers, and pattern number 9850 is for warm winter coats. Sew, pull out your machine and start stitching!

"Scarlet O'Hairy"

The First-Ever Collector Doll in the Great Litterature Series from The Bradfur Exchange. The world's most beloved heroine romantically pawtrayed in a finely crafted pawcelain collector doll. Generations have been captivated by the vivacity and style of the Southern belle, Scarlet O'Hairy. Now you can purrchase a limited-edition, one-of-a-kind pawcelain collector doll.

- -

THE BRADFUR EXCHANGE

9345 Milkdrinkers Avenue   Niles, Illinois 60606-0606

THE *Heart and Soul* OF COLLECTING

YES. Please enter my bid for Scarlet O'Hairy.* We will sell this priceless example of craftscatship to the highest bidder. SEND NO MONEY NOW. You will be billed if your doll is shipped. *Limit: only one doll has been made.*

Please Respond Promptly

*Plus a total of $3.69 postage and handling. Illinois residents add state sales tax. Doll stand not included.

Pawprint _____

Name _____

Address _____

City _____ State ____ Zip _____

Telephone (____) _____

Take a Walk on the Wild Side

Rugged gear for outdoor cats that will give your wardrobe lasting style

The Green-Eyed Monster

The season's big color: bright green, here in a slim and shapely quilted jumpsuit. Worn with a matching green nylon collar adorned with bells. The purrfect look for stalking your prey. Premier Pet Products. Catnip fish from L. Coffey Ltd.

Biker Babe

The newest look for cats on the go is this black motorcycle jacket, complete with studs, embroidered patches, and a matching cap. Hit the road! Razz Pe' Tazz.

Blanket Warmth
Blanket-plaid woolen jacket, lined with faux sherpa fur, sports a snuggly-warm hood. Razz Pe' Tazz.

Check This Out
Buffalo-check jacket and matching hat are a smart way to dress for the cold. Razz Pe' Tazz. Bird from Metropolitan Pet.

Anti-Freeze
Polartec coat in a Southwestern inspired Aztec print keeps you warm in a high-tech way. It is worn with a matching collar. Duke's Dog's Fashions.

Denim Checks
A fitted jacket in checkered blue denim is accented by a red leatherette collar. Razz Pe' Tazz.

Down Home Dressing
A trim denim coat is lined with faux sherpa fur for extra warmth. It is worn with a safety orange collar so that you will not be mistaken for prey in the woods. Premier Pet Products. Niche Pet Products collar. Vermont Home Grown catnip cow from Doggie Styles & Kittie Too!!

KITTY GLITTER
The Best Accessories

Tie one on
a tartan bandanna adds the finishing touch. Niche Pet Products, Inc.

Hot stuff

chili-pepper printed bandanna can be worn with a matching collar and leash. Duke's Dog Fashions.

Shine on
with jeweled collars. Large, colored stones from Tanner & Dash. Diamanté Pavé from Allison Craig Rare Petware.

Ultrasuede
is ultrachic when worn with a Chanel-inspired chain leash. UltraMouse, Ltd.

Globe-trotting kitties
will wear these international collars to all the best places. Tanner & Dash, Ltd.

Take our advice
this visor cap is the choice of cool cats everywhere. Rosedale Valley Road Gang.

Be there with bells on...
festive nylon collars ring in the season. Premier Pet Products.

Sparkle plenty
in rhinestone-trimmed collars. Allison Craig Rare Petware.

sheer without fur

Beautifully sheer.
Deceptively strong.
Resists snagging.

RESISTANCE
HOSIERY

Healthy Cats

BY NANCY SNYDERCAT, D.V.M.

Squeaky Clean

Q. I am a scrupulously clean cat. Some of my friends say that I am almost obsessive about my grooming. I can't stand the feel or even the idea of dirt and germs on my coat. I have noticed that I am developing bald spots on my paws, where I seem to be washing the most. Is there a connection between my cleanliness and my apparent baldness?

A. From your description, I believe that you may have a greater problem than baldness. You appear to be exhibiting a case of compulsive overgrooming, which has resulted in hair loss on your paws. The pattern you explain in your note is consistent with an emotional disorder that may require attention from a veterinarian, animal behaviorist, or both.

I recommend that you visit your veterinarian for a complete physical to rule out medical causes for your problems (baldness and overgrooming). Once a medical cause has been eliminated (as I believe will be the case), you would be wise to seek the counsel of a trained and experienced behaviorist. Good luck, and I hope you will feel better soon.

Help for Stress

Q. For many years I was an only cat, living with a family of humans. Last year one of their children brought home a stray cat. The family soon discovered that the cat was expecting a litter of kittens. They were so cute that the family decided to keep them. And before I knew it, I was sharing my home with five other cats. The pressure has been intense. The young cats get into everything, and I have to remain alert at all times to retain my position of power in the family. I seem to have a constant cold, and my stomach is always upset. I've been so stressed that I have been unable to groom myself as often as I used to. I feel like I'm coming apart at the seams. What's wrong with me?

A. I can see from your letter that you have been under a tremendous amount of stress for the past year. The symptoms you describe are consistent with stress-based ailments, which are very real and require immediate attention. If left untreated, stress can manifest itself in a number of ways, including the chronic respiratory and intestinal infections you have described. Additional symptoms may include soiling, marking, and the inadequate grooming that is mentioned in your letter.

It is imperative that you seek immediate veterinary treatment to alleviate your symptoms and to help you better cope with the pressures in your life that have precipitated the illness. Your family veterinarian may prescribe Valium to reduce your stress and remedy your symptoms. Make an appointment to see him soon.

Fat Cat Remedy

Q. I am embarrassed to admit that I am a fat cat. I mean really fat. I'm a compulsive eater. I prefur people food, like tuna and chicken and cheeseburgers. But I like cat food, too. I'm not very picky about what I eat. At first my people found it amusing that I would eat whatever they offered me. I think they viewed Morris, that finicky cat on TV, as the norm. I'm really more of a Garfield. My veterinarian didn't believe my problem. It seems that he's had thin cats his whole life, and he laid the blame on the people I live with. But it wasn't their fault. It was me. Help me. I don't know what to do.

A. I empathize with your problem. I, too, have been heavy on occasion. The first step to a solution is to radically alter your diet. You must eliminate all people food, as this is what has made you fat in the first place. I know that their food is tasty and tempting, but abstinence is your only choice. Cat food is specially formulated to provide you with a perfectly balanced diet. There are even specially designed, low-cal foods that can help you to maintain a healthy lifestyle.

Your letter does not mention any physical activity, and I believe that this oversight is not accidental. You must incorporate exercise into your daily routine to burn excess calories and aid you in achieving your ideal weight. I wish you the best of luck in making these radical changes. You are ready to take on the challenge. I hope you succeed.

Fade-Out

Q. I am a dark haired-cat who enjoys time spent outdoors. I have always been proud of my glossy black coat, but I have begun to notice that my hair seems to be losing its color. My fur has taken on a rusty red tone. I can't imagine what is going on. How can I stop this change? And is there any way to restore my hair back to its original dark color?

A. There can be several reasons for the sudden change in your hair color. You neglected to mention your age. Hair can lose pigmentation as you grow older. But if your hair is, in fact, turning red, it maybe lightening from exposure to the sun. The solution is to limit your time in the sun. Eventually your hair will return to its natural color.

The more serious explanation is that something is interfering with your hair's pigmentation process. Pigmentation can be adversely affected by malnutrition, poor diet, parasites, or hormonal abnormalities. It will require an examination from your veterinarian to determine the actual cause of your problem. I recommend that you seek competent medical attention to get to the root of the matter.

ATTENTION: YOU WILL
NEVER BE A KITTEN AGAIN, BUT YOU DON'T
HAVE TO TELL YOUR FEET.

FLEA GEAR
THEY'RE ON YOUR
FEET

Classic
Pussyfooting

Pussyfooting
Suede

Pussyfooting
Mylar

Pussyfooting
Canvas

Pussyfooting
Pearlized

Pussyfooting, about $30. Available at select pet stores, or call 1-800-FLEABAG for more information. ©1995 FLEA Gear, Inc.

Cats Who Ignore Women
and the Women Who Love Them.

Fluffy is your average cat, if any cat can be described as average. She shares her home with a single woman who leaves for work at 8:00 each weekday morning. For ten blessed hours Fluffy has the run of the apartment, amusing herself in any way she chooses. She eats when she feels like it; looks out the window when she is in the mood; plays with her many toys: the woman's makeup on the bathroom counter, the glass figurines (OOPS) on

"Why can't they leave us alone?"

the coffee table, the loose threads on the arm of the sofa; and, when all of this activity becomes too exhausting, she naps. You might say that Fluffy has a purrfect life. But you would be wrong.

At 6:00 each weekday evening, Fluffy hears the metallic sound of a key in the lock. She must sprint from wherever she is standing (or sitting, or lying) to the safety zone far underneath the woman's queen-size bed. She must next endure the sight of the woman's face, pressed against the carpeted floor, blowing kisses, "meowing" (if you can call it that) in her best catlike tones, and beseeching her to come out from under the bed. Fluffy rolls her eyes in disgust. When will this embarrassing display end? Why won't the woman go away? When will she ever learn that this is

no way to win our affection?

Fluffy is not the only cat who must endure revolting demonstrations of affection by the obviously love-starved women who live with them. Their fawning may take many forms, but the result is the same. We are repulsed by their needy demeanor, and repelled by their lavish show of atten-

tion. How can these women solve their despurrate need to smother the cats they purrport to love?

Good Mousekeeping posed this question to two renowned feline experts (who happen to be women, but we won't hold this shortcoming against them) in an effort to learn the human purrspective on this issue. We spoke

Your Problem

(continued from page 44)

with Carole Wilbourn, the renowned cat therapist, and Anitra Frazier, the famed proponent of natural cat care. Their observations and recommendations were enlightening, and in the interest of female/feline harmony, we would like to share them with you.

Carole Wilbourn's credentials are impressive. The author of four books (*Cats on the Couch, Cat Talk, The Inner Cat,* and *Cats Prefer it This Way*), an audio-cassette (*The Cat Caring Tape*), and a monthly column for *CAT FANCY* magazine ("Cats on the Couch"), she has appeared as a guest on many television and radio shows to discuss all aspects of feline behavior. She maintains a private practice in New York and is available in purrson or by phone to consult on a variety of cat-related problems. We recently spoke with her about this problem, which seems prevalent among the women who live with cats. She offered the following advice to those despurrate, misdirected women.

"Yes, it doesn't surprise me that your cat seems to act in an *au contraire* way. I think that the following tip will ingratiate you with your cat. Instead of throwing yourself at her (or him—male cats can suffer from identical abuse), use your feminine wiles. Be provocative. Be seductive. If you want your cat to come to you or play with a particular toy, don't scream and yell for your cat to come over. Instead, concentrate on the toy in a lighthearted fashion and make it intriguing. Don't be surprised if your cat shows up to get in on the action.

"If you want your cat to grace your lap, go into your bedroom and stretch out on the bed. Your body and spirit will completely relax, and you will soon find your cat beside you.

"Remember, cats love the hunt. Mystery is their second nature. Seductiveness becomes them."

Anitra Frazier has long been recognized as one of this country's leading authorities on natural cat care. She is the author of the groundbreaking works *The Natural Cat* and *The New Natural Cat*, which explore the holistic treatment of felines. Ms. Frazier is a contributing editor to *Tiger Tribe* magazine, and she maintains a private practice, consulting with patients in purrson or by phone on a wide variety of issues that may be improved through holistic care. We recently presented her with the problem posed by Fluffy to seek her expert advice. She first addresses Fluffy in an effort to achieve harmony.

"Your human is reaching for much-needed affection. If you can make her feel loved and wanted, she will be satisfied and not so needy all of the time. I understand that you may be more sensitive, she may not be aware of what is more pleasant to you.

"Wait until she is asleep and crawl into bed with her. You can give her your warmth and tranquil purring and not be subject to unwanted petting. Be sure to wake up first, and be sure that she is aware that you have been there all night.

"I suggest grooming around her ear with a rough tongue. She'll wake up with a giggle. You can continue around her hairline (if she doesn't use hairspray!)."

Ms. Frazier offers the following advice to women who have problems expressing their affection toward their cats in a nonaggressive way.

"You must realize that one reason you love cats is that they express affection differently than we do. If your cat is in the room asleep, this means she trusts you. Otherwise she'd have her eyes open and her ears pulled back. Because they are so much more sensitive than we are, cats don't need to wrap their legs around us in a hug to show their affection. Looking into our eyes and executing a slow blink is the equivalent of a cat's kiss.

"If you want to get a really positive response from your cat, instead of stroking and scrumpling the fur in a forceful manner, try petting—keeping your hand a half inch away from the cat at all times—without touching her. Petting her aura. You'll soon have your cat pressing against your hand for more. In other words, pull back and let your cat come to you."

We agree with all of the advice offered by these experts. While it is difficult for us to tolerate the groveling of these despurrate women, we must step back and see the situation from their less-enlightened purrspective. It is only then that we can learn to exercise a bit of constraint and acceptance for individuals who are not as fortunate as we are. Purrhaps, in time, they will understand that we do, in fact, love them, but in our own special way. ★

THE QUESTION IS NOT WHY BUY GOLD FROM CTV.

*b*uying gold is not something you do every day. It's also something most of us don't know much about. So how can you make sure that you're not buying anything less than the best?

Start by asking questions.

Will the retailer guarantee the quality in writing? Will they affix their pawprint to the receipt? Will they offer a 30-day unconditional money-back guarantee? If your retailer is CTV (Cat-TV), the answer to all of these questions is yes.

We won't stop until you have all the answers.

Asking questions is a good start, but to ensure the highest quality possible, you have to go even further.

Which is exactly what CTV does. We go directly to the manufacturers to make sure each piece of jewelry stands up to our strict standards—from purity and craftscatship to finish and consistency. We regularly visit hundreds of workshops, all over the world, to find the best designs and craftscatship. Hardly anybody else does that. But we're not just anybody. We're cats, and we're Cat-TV.

Nobody has the kind of infurmation CTV has.

At CTV, one of America's largest retailers of jewelry for cats, we know more about the pieces we sell than anyone else. We think it's critical that you know everything, too. Because when you buy jewelry, you're doing more than just picking out something pretty. You're making a purrchase that should last nine lifetimes.

That's why we do everything catly possible to make sure the jewelry you buy from us not only gives you the highest quality today, but for lifetimes to come. So when it comes to buying cat jewelry from someone you can trust, the choice is obvious. CTV. No question.

CTV

MORRIS

A Rats-to-Riches Tale of How I Clawed My Way to the Top of the Corpurrate Ladder

BY MORRIS

Every morning I awaken and survey the view of green lawns from my bedroom window. I pay particularly close attention to the nearest tree, home to a perky bird. I've spent hours observing. My stomach grumbles when I suddenly remember that my life has dramatically changed. Six A.M. Time to remind my valet, who works the can opener, that it's time for my 9-Lives Plus breakfast. My days of roughing it with other strays on the tough streets of Chicago are behind me.

How did I escape life on the streets? After being abandoned, I was rescued by a humane society, where I spent some time with other homeless cats and dogs. Dogs—don't get me started. But anyway, I always knew I had a distinct purrsonality, even if the other felines thought I was being catty. I knew that I was destined for greatness. A home of my own, a bowl full of 9-Lives, my own press agent. But in the meantime I made the most of my time at the shelter, wooing the staff with my charm and keeping the dogs in line. I patiently waited for the world to discover what I already knew—that I was a diamond in the rough just waiting to be found!

Oh sure, sometimes when the other cats would go home with their new humans I would wonder why it was taking so long for my ship to come in. I suppose to some people my incredible good looks and finicky attitude were intimidating. Those soft, fluffy kittens who kept getting picked, in my opinion, didn't hold a candle to me. But I never gave up hope. Humans can be slow, but if you wait long enough, they'll do the right thing most of the time. Besides, I was kind of enjoying being the boss around the place.

After a while a woman came to meet me. I studied her closely from the corner of my eyes. I feigned disinterest. She looked directly at me and smiled. I yawned and turned away.

She approached and gently extended her hand in my direction. I sniffed it warily and met her gaze. I kept my cool. Not bad for a human, I thought. I walked slowly toward her for a final inspection, checking her pockets for treats. I found some. She was mine.

Next, we signed the paperwork making the adoption official. After a short drive, we arrived home. She was trained very well—she immediately made me comfortable, setting out a dish of delicious shredded canned cat food, water, and a special bed. Because you have to teach humans who's boss early on, I began insisting that she include ice in my water. It took her some time, but she finally learned the trick.

Anyway, back to my first day at home. I was just about to go to sleep when she sat down at the table and dialed a number. Unfortunately, it interrupted my cat nap.

Sensing this was important, I leaned forward to listen as she began chattering into the phone. "I found him. I found Morris! He's perfect," she said gleefully. Who's Morris? I thought. I don't know anyone by that name. It certainly wasn't me.

Before I could begin my lecture on the fact that she must have mistaken me for another cat, she swept me into a large carrying case and we were on our way to the city.

When we arrived, I was surprised that everything was so clean and bright. She carried me into a tall building with lots of windows, and we stepped into a tiny

room. The doors slid closed and I had the uneasy sensation of moving quickly upward. In a couple of moments we jolted to a stop. The doors slid open again and we stepped out.

She walked up to a big desk where another woman was sitting. "I'm here with Morris," she said distinctly. Who's Morris? I thought again. I'll have to speak with her about this later.

She carried me into a large room and shut the door. She placed my carrier on a long table and finally opened the latch. I stepped out into the bright sunlight. As I blinked my eyes to adjust to the light, I observed that I was in an elegantly appointed, wood-paneled room. They sure didn't have rooms like this at the humane society! I had never seen such a grand room before, but I immediately knew I was born to live in such luxury.

I was standing on a long wooden table, its surface polished to a high sheen. I walked toward the end of the table and noticed that my paws had left little marks tracing my footsteps. Pretty neat, I thought. I'll leave tracks wherever I go. I glanced toward the windows and saw that the curtains were drawn open, providing a clear view of the city below. I had never been up so high, and the people on the street beneath me looked like mice. I was just getting comfortable with my new surroundings when several people walked excitedly into the room.

I glanced up, stretched, and realized that every eye was on me. Everyone was smiling. Then one of them pulled a cloth off an easel that was sitting at the front of the room. There, underneath that cloth, was a large photograph of the most attractive cat I had ever seen. What a handsome fellow, I thought. Then I realized something—that picture was of me! Or someone who looked like me. Well, whatever the case, at least they have good taste, I thought.

I sat down and glanced at all the interested faces staring at me. What are they all looking at? I thought, haven't you ever seen a cat as good-looking as I?

The group retreated back to their seats, and they spoke quietly among themselves. Then they spoke to the woman, and she seemed pleased. She came over to me and said "I know that

you've had a very strange day. First I have taken you from everything that was familiar and I have brought you to this place. Let me assure you that everything from now on will be good. You are safe, and you will lead a happy and fulfilling life. My name is Dawn, and I will be your companion and teacher. I know the shelter called you by another name, but we will be calling you Morris, Morris III, to be exact. You are the third cat to uphold the fine tradition that was begun in 1968. At that time, a stray orange cat, much like yourself, was adopted from a

shelter in Hinsdale, Illinois. That cat had great presence and personality, much like yourself. I saw it immediately in you at the shelter. You stood out from all the other cats...."

Well, I agreed wholeheartedly with the young lady. I was, of course, a claw above the rest of my shelter friends. And I sat and listened to what became a very

interesting story about my predecessors and the paws I would have to fill.

Dawn went on to describe the glorious life that the first Morris had led as spokescat for 9-Lives. He was known as the "King of Cat Food," and, after winning the plum assignment over thousands of hopefuls, spent the next 11 years traveling and meeting with people on behalf of his favorite cat food.

Morris II was found in a New England animal shelter in 1980 after an exhausting search across the country for a cat capable of living up to the

high standards set by his predecessor. Morris II continued in the footsteps of the first Morris, appearing on television with world famous celebrities (much like himself) on shows such as *Lifestyles of the Rich and Famous*, *Good Morning America*, *Entertainment Tonight*, and *Oprah*. He was called "the feline Burt Reynolds" by *Time* maga-

MORRIS
The 9 Lives PLUS Cat

"I always knew I had a distinct purrsonality, even if the other felines thought I was being catty."

zine and selected by *Young Miss Magazine (YM)* as one of the world's most admired males.

I learned that despite the glamorous image, Morris had always been a philanthropist at heart. For many years he took time out of his hectic schedule to serve as spokescat for Adopt-A-Cat Month, which benefited the American Humane Association and 1,000 animal shelters nationwide. And for five years, he served as spokescat for Cat Health Month, sponsored by Heinz Pet Products and the American Veterinary Medical Association.

He used his charm, media savvy, and fame to teach cat owners to treat their feline friends the way he liked to be treated. He was "up in paws" that many cats didn't get the regular checkups and inoculations that they needed, so he starred in a number of televised public

service announcements concerning cat health. He also wrote two books on cat health and behavior, *The Morris Prescription* and *The Morris Method.*

In 1988 and again in 1992, Morris campaigned to be elected as President of the United States, taking Washington by storm and rallying millions of loyal supporters. Although polls showed that he had greater name recognition than all other candidates except George Bush, he withdrew from the race to return to the cat food business and philanthropy full time. And then, after 15 years as spokescat for 9-Lives, he retired with his handler, Bob Martwick, to a life of leisure. Today he spends his days relaxing at home, in excellent health, and eating his favorite flavors of 9-Lives cat food.

After hearing this inspurrational tale, I agreed to uphold the fine tradition set by those who came before. With my

dazzling purrsonality and good looks I knew it would be an easy fit. Now I wear the Morris name proudly. I have already made several television commercials for my favorite cat food, the new shredded varieties. I have made purrsonal appearances and participated in media interviews. My favorite part so far has been the pictures. Besides the fact that I am a pretty handsome fellow, I've noticed that most of the photo opportunities involve me posing with my favorite foods. It's great to get in an extra meal now and again!

Most recently I launched the P.L.U.S. (Protect and Love Us!) campaign to encourage cat owners to care responsibly for their cats. Part of that responsibility includes proper feeding, which has prompted me to actively support the exciting new line of 9-Lives Plus canned cat food. It's truly a labor of love: I love the five new shredded flavors best of all.

Dawn was right. My life is very good (but I deserve it). When I'm not in front of the cameras or cheering crowds, I stay at home in Chicago with Dawn. Even though she's a human, she's a great companion. I spend my free time purrfecting my finicky attitude for the cameras and watching the birds outside my window. Only today, I watch birds purely as sport. I much prefurr dining on 9-Lives Plus. ★

AT HOME WITH MOUSER STEWART

America's do-it-yourself queen invited *Good Mousekeeping* to visit her at her opulent Connecticut estate, Mousy Hill Farm. She generously shares her home with several other feline relatives.

"Meet my brother, Chaz. He was the last one who came to stay, and I'm afraid that all of the masculine bedrooms were already taken. If he stays much longer, I'll just have to redecorate."

"I love to make all of my guests feel at home in whatever room they choose, so I have placed comfortable, but stylish, beds in every room of my house," she said, leading us into her immense living room. "Parlor. I prefer to call it a parlor. That is the correct formal term. You will notice my aunt, Peaches, reclining on the green couch."

"We are passing through the foyer. I have decorated this room so that it can also serve as a library. You will notice my sister Pia, in the faux-leopard nest bed. Oh, Pia, I'm sorry we've awakened you with the lights and photo equipment. She's so sensitive. You'd think that she'd be used to the camera crews by now."

"This is my media room, I mean family room. The cozy decor is conducive to warm evenings spent gathered around the glue gun, fashioning clever trinkets to be featured in my magazine, Mouser Stewart's Living Well is the Best Revenge. You've seen it on all the newsstands, haven't you? Meet my cousin, Miss Kitty. I'm sorry that the cameras are blocking your view of the television, but we won't be another moment, dear."

"We are in one of my many guest bedrooms. It's amazing that once you have cultivated a reputation for entertaining graciously, so many guests have the unpleasant habit of coming to visit and expecting to stay! I have therefore added a wing to my home for these frequent boarders. The guest rooms are decorated as lavishly as the rest of my home, because I look upon interior design as a reflection of my own personal taste. And my taste is superb. Uncle Louie, we were just leaving."

"This is my daughter's room. Oliver, we call her Ollie, is reclining in a pink satin cushion that I have cleverly set upon an antique four-poster bed. It is never too early to cultivate an appreciation for the finer things. You will also notice that her collar spells out "cat" in French. Trés Jolie!"

"Please come into my bedroom. Barguzin, what are you doing here? Meet my sister Bargie. Well, you may as well stay for the picture because this cheap magazine did not provide a hair and makeup person, and my contract stipulates that I will not appear on camera without one. Stretch out on the bed, but don't dirty the sheets with your feet."

"This is my bathroom. I didn't realize that someone was in here! It's my ex-husband, Randy Jake! How long have you been living here? Since our divorce? Well, just be sure to put the seat down when you're through. Where was I? Oh, yes. Thank you and all of the Good Mousekeeping readers for visiting my humble home. And don't forget to read my magazine and watch my show on TV."

Paws to Catch Your Breath:
FAT CATS
Go for the Burn

"Should I sit in the living room and stalk the birds in the cage? Should I unravel the yarn in her new sweater? Maybe I'll scratch the arms of the sofa again. So many things, so little time. What to do?"

Kitty-Go-Round

Stress. We all know that feeling of anxiety that comes over us when we have too many things to accomplish at once. How we wish that we could organize our days, and our *lives*, so that we could get everything done and achieve a feeling of accomplishment.

All it takes is a system. The easiest path to purrsonal well-being is to make time for the things that are important. We must learn to set our priorities. Our schedule should include time for each activity in order of importance: eating, sleeping, and exercise. **Exercise?**

We know how that word makes you shudder with repulsion. Cats. Exercise. The two concepts seem to be at odds. Yet, when you examine some of the activities that bring you pleasure, such as the ones listed at the beginning of this article, you'll have to admit that they *are* a form of physical activity. Hence, we can apply the socially acceptable term *exercise* to them. And by calling these enjoyable activities exercise, we can justify a lot of our destructive actions.

People make strange household companions. They do not take pleasure in many of the things we enjoy most. Have you ever seen the expression on a woman's face when we bestow upon her our highest honor and present her with a freshly caught mouse? Talk about repulsion...

Yet humans provide us with a number of advantages that cannot be overlooked, including a warm and comfortable home, a wealth of good places to sleep, plenty

Jungle Kitty Gym

Stretch your paws
(left) You'll soon feel the benefits of this simple activity, that is often overlooked. Try batting at a ball on a wire, like the one shown here. The repetitive motion builds stamina and endurance. Kitty-Go-Round from M&M Enterprises.

Expect the unexpected
(above) A Jungle Kitty Gym, like the one shown here, is constructed with a variety of stimuli that can be activated at once. You never know what to expect, a philosophy that also can be applied to life. Jungle Kitty Gym from OLT International.

Never underestimate the benefits of looking good
(right) This cleverly designed piece of exercise equipment combines the stimulation of motion with the benefits of massage and a good brushing. You emerge looking good and feeling good. Feline Fantasy Brush from M&M Enterprises.

Feline Fantasy Brush

Kitty Tumbler Tunnel

of regular meals, and a house filled with opportunities for stimulating physical activity. The benefits far outweigh the costs. And once we apply a little bit of human psychology to the equation, the results are unbeatable.

Our primary objective is to purrform the activities we enjoy most without provoking the anger of our human companions. We must walk a delicate line to reconcile these differences to our mutual satisfaction. This is easier to accomplish than you think. Cats are known for their sense of balance and resourcefulness. We must apply a positive spin to things we choose to do, turning them into actions that people will accept and respect.

Humans have spent untold time and money to devise toys that replicate our favorite forms of prey and can substitute for our most cherished activities. Looking back at the wish list that began this article, the joy derived from stalking birds can be transfurred to stalking feathery, birdlike devices. Similarly, scratching a sisal- or carpet-covered post until our paws are exhausted is a good substitute for shredding a sweater or the arm of a sofa. We achieve the same sense of accomplishment while our people smile and marvel at how much *exercise* we are getting from the toys they've purrchased. Everyone wins.

Most of all, enjoy it

We're only here for a short time (nine lives, and counting), so we should reach right in with four paws and take hold of everything life has to offer. And if we can leave the good stuff undamaged when we're through, we'll be happy cats living with happy people. ★

Krinkle Sack

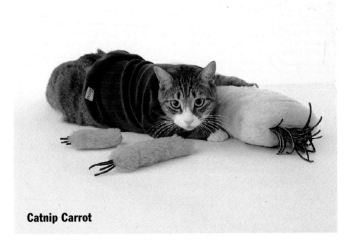

Catnip Carrot

FELINE FITNESS

How to Choose *the Right Toys for Working Out*

We've seen many cats quit exercising because they've chosen the wrong toys. Some toys are boring and lack the elements that should attract us to them in the first place.

A good toy must be a treat for all of the senses. It should be colorful, textural, tasty, and durable, with a pleasant sound and fun to use. It should not contain any sharp or dangerous parts that could break off and be swallowed.

Because we possess a short attention span, it is important to select an assortment of interesting toys. A key piece of advice: show your people how much you enjoy playing with your toys. This will guarantee an endless supply of new toys in your future.

A New Toy Review
GM comments on a selection of new toys from some of the most popular companies.

Plush Catnip-Filled Lobster:
Nip & Tuck Playtoys
Soft, plush surface
Fragrant, fresh catnip filling
Toy has a Velcro™ closure and is refillable

Assortment of Catnip-Filled Sushi:
Maggie Mae's Gourmet Pet Products
Soft, fuzzy surface
Fragrant catnip filling
Amusing assortment of shapes

Audubon Bird
Metropolitan Pet
Intricately detailed, stuffed cloth bird
Attached to heavy wire on acrylic rod
Wings flap for realistic effect

Kittybird
Kittybird, Inc.
Unique and colorful cat toy
Made of turkey feathers colored with nontoxic dyes
Base is weighted with sawdust

Cat Charmer
Cat Dancer Products, Inc.
Safe, interactive toy for all cats and kittens
Colorful, durable fabric attached to acrylic rod
Excellent aerobic exercise device

Garfield
UP CLOSE AND PURRSONAL

Good Mousekeeping Gets The Scoop...

He's fat, he's lazy, and he has a grumpy disposition. For all these reasons and more, we love Garfield, the world's most hilarious cat. Born in the kitchen of Mama Leone's Italian restaurant in 1978, Garfield has grown into a worldwide (and we do mean *wide*) celebrity. His antics with his hapless owner, Jon Arbuckle, his faithful friend and whipping dog, Odie, and his beloved teddy bear, Pooky, bring laughter to millions daily.

But what's so appealing about a tubby tabby with a rude attitude? What

makes Garfield so lovable? It's simple...Cats relate to him because he *is* them. Garfield loves TV and hates Mondays. He'd rather pig out than work out. In fact, his passion for food and sleep is matched only by his aversion to diet and exercise (he prefers lay-downs to sit-ups). He'd like mornings better if they started later. What could be more feline?

Cats also enjoy and identify with Garfield's sassy brand of humor. Garfield is quick-witted, and the first to admit it. He never hesitates to say the things that cats would like to say, in a way they'd like to say them. But he's

never socially unacceptable, just tastefully outrageous. Because, after all, "maturity is overrated."

But Garfield is not all sass and sarcasm; he also has a soft side. He really loves his teddy bear, Pooky, and deep down, he loves Jon and Odie, too (just not as much as he loves himself, of course).

Garfield is also quite the business-cat. Since his introduction in newspaper comics in 1978, his comic strip now appears in over 2,500 newspapers worldwide, making it the fastest growing strip in history. It wasn't long before the popular and critically acclaimed comic strip mushroomed into a library of publishing successes, Emmy-award-winning, prime-time animated TV specials, and more than 3,500 Garfield licensed products worldwide.

When it comes to publishing accomplishments, Garfield wrote the book, beginning with his first in 1980, *Garfield at Large*. To date, 33 Garfield titles, published by Ballantine books, have appeared on the *New York Times* and other notable bestseller lists, with 11 titles hitting the number-one spot on the *New York Times* list and seven titles appearing simultaneously in 1983.

One of Garfield's favorite pastimes, besides eating and sleeping, is watching TV. So it was only natural that the curmudgeonly cat would take to the tube. His first animated prime-time special, "Here Comes Garfield," debuted on CBS in 1982. It has been followed by 13 more, and their popularity led to the creation of a weekly series, *Garfield and Friends*, which airs on CBS on Saturday mornings.

The great orange cat took to the stage in 1986 to present *Garfield's Furry Tales*, and *Garfield's Magic Show*. These have been joined by other productions purrformed at community theatres, symphony halls, malls, zoos, and community festivals all over the country.

Garfield has also been riding high, as a giant helium balloon, seen in parades all across the country. His favorite may be his annual appearance over the Macy's Thanksgiving Day Parade, which is seen by millions both in person and on television.

Yet, despite the heavy demands on his time by his corpurrate responsibilities, Garfield finds time in his busy schedule to give something back to his fellow felines. A firm believer in feline philanthropy, Garfield has appeared in public service announcements, which advocate cat care, produced by the Humane Society of the United States (HSUS).

Garfield has also begun work on a theme park near Indianapolis, Indiana. He will be the host and star of the Garfield Zone, located in the park, which will celebrate the state of Indiana and midwestern heritage.

Garfield's pet project for 1996 grew out of his thought, "Isn't it time to put a REAL fat cat in the White House?" He has announced his candidacy for President, putting fear into the heart of Socks Clinton, who has grown complacent with the passive title of "First Cat." "America needs Garfield," he boasts, and besides, "you've done worse!" ★

Good Mousekeeping Speaks With Garfield Purrsonal & Up Close

GM: How old are you?

Garfield: I was born on June 19, 1978, so I am now 18. This is a milestone birthday. I'll be celebrating all year long. As I always say, anything worth doing is worth overdoing.

GM: Did Jon adopt you from a shelter?

Garfield: No, Jon purchased me from a pet store. Whatever he paid it wasn't anywhere near what I'm worth. But I shouldn't complain. Jon did give me a comfortable home. At the pet shop I lived with a lizard and a hamster with a hacking cough.

GM: How does it feel to be a celebrity?

Garfield: I love the fame and attention. And I've finally got the six-figure food budget I always wanted. But I do miss the privacy. Seems like I can't whack Odie or insult Jon without it hitting the newspapers.

GM: What are some things that people can do to make their cats happy?

Garfield: Cater to their every whim. Ban dogs. Get cable. Change the kitty litter. And keep the fridge full. That should do it.

GM: What do you think are the biggest problems that cats face today? Do you have any advice on how to cope with these problems?

Garfield: Well, we definitely have a cat population problem. In other words, there are way too many pets that aren't cats. We need to educate the public about this. Cat abuse is also a serious problem. Cats are being asked to dance, play with string, wear funny hats on home videos. It's appalling. Cats are not animals; they're pets! Also, we need to develop a refrigerator with a pet door. I'm not sure how to solve any of these problems; we'd better sleep on them.

GM: Are cats smarter than dogs?

Garfield: Rocks are smarter than dogs. Next question.

GM: How much do you weigh?

Garfield: Let's just say that when I tip the scales, they stay tipped. Still, I'm not overweight; I'm undertall.

GM: What do you do for exercise?

Garfield: I try to watch at least 30 minutes of exercise every day. Then I follow it with a brisk two-hour nap.

GM: How do you feel about a cat being in the White House?

Garfield: It's great that we have a First Feline. Too many of our presidents have been unduly influenced by the canine lobby. Of course, I won't be satisfied until cats are actually running things. I, for instance, would make an outstanding Chief Exalted Ruler of the Universe.

Garfield's Likes and Dislikes

LIKES

- sleep ("Too much sleep is never enough.")
- being lazy ("Some call it laziness. I call it deep thought.")
- self-indulgence ("If you don't indulge yourself, who will?")
- pigging-out ("Never put off till tomorrow what you can eat today.")
- weekends ("Wake me for the weekend.")
- parties ("Only on days ending in *y*.")
- food ("The best things in life are edible.")
- remote control ("Greatest invention since the can opener.")
- my weight ("I'm the perfect shape for my weight.")

DISLIKES

- diets ("Too little of a good thing. Diet is *die* with a *t*.")
- exercise ("I consider it a spectator sport. My favorite exercise is a brisk nap.")
- mornings ("They should start later.")
- chasing mice ("Show me a good mouser, and I'll show you a cat with bad breath.")
- modesty ("It's hard to be humble when you're as great as I am.")
- Jon's wardrobe ("It's right out of GQ...*Geek's Quarterly*.")
- cooking ("I'm an eater, not a cooker.")
- work ("You couldn't pay me to work.")
- an empty stomach ("Never overlook the obvious.")

It takes a special mouse to win the admiration of the entire cat population. Few mice have earned our love, much less respect. The vast majority of cats who responded to our recent *Good Mousekeeping* survey voted Mickey Mouse their favorite mouse.

Aside from the few votes cast for mice caught by our readers in their own homes, it was Mickey's name who appeared with overwhelming frequency on our readers' ballots. Despite the natural antipathy between cats and mice, most of our readers looked beyond the mouse package to see the character within.

Many readers felt compelled to supplement their survey form with written notes to explain their selection. Several readers were impressed with the

running a Mickey. Soon theaters were displaying posters that read "Mickey Mouse playing today!"

When the United States entered World War II, Disney suspended nearly all commercial activity and concentrated on aiding the war effort with training films and goodwill tours, designing posters and armed forces insignia. Mickey urged Americans to buy war bonds. And, incredibly, the password of the Allied forces on D-day, June 6, 1944, was "Mickey Mouse."

Following the war, Mickey returned to making cartoons and appeared in his second feature, *Fun and Fancy Free*, in 1947.

After the success of the *Disneyland* television show in 1954, Disney agreed the next year to create an afternoon

Mickey Mouse

Our Most Beloved Mouse

motivation that drove a humble mouse to achieve fame and fortune as the star of stage and screen. Others recognized his superior managerial skills, which propelled him up the Disney corpurrate ladder to lofty heights. Still others alluded to his humble demeanor and good taste. So many of our readers expressed an interest in learning more about their favorite rodent that *Good Mousekeeping* contacted the Walt Disney Company to find out the whole tale.

Mickey was born in Walt Disney's imagination early in 1928 on a train ride from New York to Los Angeles. Walt was returning with his wife from a business meeting at which his cartoon creation, Oswald the Rabbit, had been wrested from him by his financial backers.

Walt spent the return trip conjuring up a little mouse in red velvet pants and named him Mortimer, but by the time the train screeched into the terminal in Los Angeles, the dream mouse had been renamed. Walt's wife, Lillian, thought the name Mortimer was too pompous and suggested Mickey. A star was born.

Upon returning to his studio, Walt and his head animator immediately began work on the first Mickey Mouse cartoon, *Plane Crazy*. No distributor wanted to buy the film. Refusing to give up, Walt forged into production on another silent Mickey, *The Gallopin' Gaucho*. However, late in 1927 Warner Brothers ushered in the talkies with The *Jazz Singer*, starring Al Jolson. This signaled

the end of silent films, so in 1928 Walt dropped everything to begin a third Mickey cartoon, this one in sound, *Steamboat Willie*.

Steamboat Willie scored an overwhelming success, and Mickey soon became the talk of the nation.

Mickey's skyrocket to fame didn't take long. His cartoons became so popular that before buying tickets customers would ask whether the theater was

program for ABC. *The Mickey Mouse Club* became the most successful children's show ever. In 1977, *The New Mickey Mouse Club* made its debut on television.

Mickey moved to Disneyland in 1955 to become the theme park's chief host, welcoming millions of visitors annually, shaking hands, posing for pictures, and leading the big parades on national holidays.

His other activities include public appearance tours for the studios. In 1971, he helped to open Walt Disney World in central Florida, and in 1983 he even donned a kimono for Tokyo Disneyland. More recently, he had to brush up on his French to greet guests at Disneyland Paris.

Why is he so popular? He was a little guy born out of the Depression who satirized our foibles and taught us how to laugh. Most importantly, he was a character who dared to dream big, and his dreams were realized. We all know how much cats appreciate a good nap and dream!

One of the finest tributes to Mickey was paid by Walt Disney himself when he surveyed Disneyland on his first TV show and said, "I hope we never lose sight of one fact...that this was all started by a mouse."

It is for all these reasons and more that we are proud to bestow upon our rodent friend the high honor of *Good Mousekeeping's* Favorite Mouse. ★

LITTER MATTERS

Cats Camp Out

Camping out is a wonderful activity to share with your kittens. A number of innovative products will make your explorations of the great outdoors safe and enjoyable.

The first thing to purrchase is a sturdy tent. *Good Mousekeeping* has seen several models. Our favorites are the Aztec-printed tent from Duke's Dog Fashions and the blue nylon Play Time pup tent from Johnson Pet-Dor. The printed tent is smaller than the blue one, so choose the size that you need. Both set up easily, but the blue tent comes with a storage and travel bag.

The outdoors can be dangerous, especially at night. Special collars have been designed so that you and your kittens can be seen in the dark. This will help prevent you from being struck down by passing vehicles. You should wear a bright reflective collar like the safety orange one from Niche Pet Products. Two other good choices are the light-up collar and safety light from Protect-a-Pet.

Identification tags are a must in case

one of your brood gets lost. These can be purrchased by mail from a variety of sources, or you can make your own tag at home using a kit from FasTags. The kit contains an ID tag in one of several different designs. You simply fill in the purrsonal information using the pen provided. Then pop the tag into the oven for five minutes, where it will shrink to it's final size. It's easy and fun to do.

Exposure to the elements can be damaging to the coat and skin. You and your kitties should apply a good sunscreen and insect repellent before braving the outdoors. Sun Spot and Bug Out are two good products to try. They are manufactured by Bio Chemics Inc. especially for pets. Both formulas come in convenient pump sprays.

Cats coming into contact with water sources should wear flotation vests. A life vest can save your life if you or one of your young falls into deep water. A life vest designed especially for pets is available from Johnson Pet-Dor. It comes in an assortment of sizes to fit every member of your family. The foam vest is just like the ones that people wear

and the safety yellow color makes it highly visible.

It is wise to take every precaution when you camp out. However, accidents can happen, so be prepared with a first-aid kit. The Pet-Aid Kit contains everything you need in case of an emergency. In addition to pet medical supplies, the kit provides first-aid instructions to help you until medical attention arrives. The kit is available from Kittybird, Inc.

Drinking flowing water is made easy when you drink from the Kitty Kreek. The device, from Tranquility Enterprises, simulates a mountain stream, providing all the same benefits without the danger. You can even set it up indoors to remind you of the fun you had during your outdoor adventures.

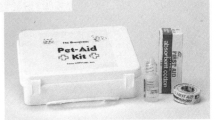

LITTER MATTERS

EDUCATIONAL TV

It's so hard to teach your children to be good feline citizens. Sometimes we wish that we could seek professional help to guide us in our task. The San Francisco SPCA has come to our aid. They have consulted with feline behaviorist

Kate Gamble to produce a series of three educational videotapes they call Cat Behavior 101.

The first tape, "What Makes Tabby Tick," explores the reasons why territory is of utmost importance to cats and why changes and threats to territory are the biggest source of cat behavior problems.

The second tape is called "Home Introductions." This tape teaches how to establish a new cat in the home, how to introduce a new cat to resident cats or other animals, and solutions for dealing with a cat's aggressive behavior toward its human companions and other cats.

The third tape is called "Correcting Bad Habits." Discover why cats scratch, spray, and stop using the litter box—and learn how to correct these problems through easy-to-follow, step-by-step instructions.

This simple home-study course nips bad behavior in the bud.

HIGH-TECH TRAINING

Active kittens have a way of getting into every-thing. You always find them where they don't belong. It's hard to train them to stay off the furniture, out of off-limits areas, and away from dangerous appliances like the stove. Don't let curiosity kill the cat. A simple electronic device has been designed to aid you in training your kittens to respect your people's property. Scraminal, from Amtek, is a harmless security system that emits a series of short, high-pitched beeps to repel your kittens from where they are not welcome. The Scraminal is a small plastic box, no larger than a transistor radio, and it is battery operated. The alarm automatically resets, so it can provide repeated warnings until your youngsters take the hint.

Stack 'EM

Litters of kittens can fill up your home pretty quickly. Space can become tight. Where will they all sleep? Flexi-Mat has solved the space problem with its bunk bed. They call it the Hammock Bed, but it is a regular bunk bed for your kittens. You need just a few to create your own dorm!

TREATS & FOOD

Cat Candy

We all deserve a little treat now and then. Okay, all the time. For those times when nothing but a treat will do, we recommend that you try one of the fish-flavored snacks from Haute Feline. Haute Feline Cat Snacks are fish shaped and taste delicious. Les Fleurettes are their newest snack food. These treats are shaped like flowers and are delicately flavored with seafood.

Special occasions call for special treats. Mullen and Fitzmaurice offer a complete line of gift packs filled with mouth-watering morsels. Their products are available in fabric sacks, pretty boxes, and beautiful gift baskets. Send one to a friend or to yourself.

Drink to Your Health

While most cats drink ordinary tap water, some cats prefer the new feline beverages that combine fresh flavor with added health benefits. Pawier comes packaged in a familiar green bottle. This clear beverage is purified water fortified with vitamins—mineral water for cats. It is available by the bottle, with its own water bowl, in self-preparation kits, first-aid and travel kits, and in beautiful gift sets and baskets.

Protect-a-Pet offers its Aloe Vera Drink, which lists many health benefits beyond those of plain water. Suzie's Pet Supplies produces Suzie's Tartar Liquid, which helps to control tartar build-up on teeth. This liquid is added to your regular drinking water, and the benefits can be seen in a short time.

The Spice of Life

Perk up your meals with zesty toppings. Toppers are gourmet sauces that you pour over your regular food. They come in several flavors, including Rack of Lamb, Chicken Teriyaki, Veggie Marinara, Shrimp Alfredo, and Turkey & Cranberry. Add a spoonful or two to your dish and taste the difference.

Sprinkles is a delicious flavor enhancer for cat foods. Packaged in a handy shaker jar, it will last for months. It is manufactured by Nickers International, who also produce several healthy products including BIO-COAT (good for glossy fur), Gentle Lax-A-Pet (a hairball eliminator), and Vite-E-Pet (a vitamin E supplement).

Louise Jane's Seafood Seasoning is another shake-on treat for cats. This product is formulated with catnip, so it is particularly addictive for those cats who react to catnip. The product is available from Kennebec River Co.

Take a Nip of Catnip

Some cats go wild for the scent or taste of catnip. Those pussies addicted to this drug will crave several catnip treats. The Kennebec River Co. offers catnip in several forms. Besides Seafood Seasoning, they supply catnip by the box (Maine Coon Cat-Nip), as well as dried catnip bouquets. Doggie Styles & Kitty Too!! offers its Vermont Home Grown Catnip in a planter, so you can grow your own.

Five ways Catfish like to travel.

Lickety Split

Incatnito

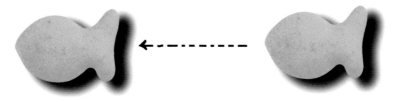

Purrposefully

On little cats fins.

In packs.

A litte fish. A lotta flavor.

Quick Cuisine

6 Meals in Minutes

*Hungry?
Want to eat
in a hurry?
Just follow
these simple
directions
for six
delicious
meals that
can be
ready in a
minute.*

Liver Pâte

A traditional favorite, popular at parties, can be ready in a flash. Set out a beautiful dish. This colorful one from Morningside Design's Multi-Cat collection is purrfect. Pop open a can of *9-Lives Liver.* Using an ice-cream scoop, form the food into a ball. Place it into the dish. Garnish with dry cat food. Serves one.

Veal in Aspic

This gourmet delight can be prepared in a moment. Set out a beautiful dish. The Purple Cat bowl from Morningside Design is a good choice. Pop open a can of *Amoré Veal in Aspic.* Place it into the dish. Garnish with cat treats. Serves one.

Beef Stew

A stick-to-the-ribs favorite, ready when you are. Set out a beautiful dish. This blue and white mouse pattern from Morningside Design is a great option. Pop open a can of *9-Lives Plus Shredded Beef.* Spoon it into the dish. Garnish with cat treats. Serves one.

Turkey in Gravy

A light but filling dinner favorite. Set out a beautiful dish. The Cat Burglar bowl from Morningside Design is a perky alternative. Pop open a can of *9-Lives Turkey Dinner.* Using an ice-cream scoop, form the food into a ball. Place it into the dish. Garnish with cat treats. Serves one.

Shrimp in Aspic

An elegant entrée for entertaining special guests, like yourself. Set out a beautiful dish. The Lime Cat bowl from Morningside Design is a striking selection. Pop open a can of *Sheba Shrimp in Aspic.* Place it into the dish. Garnish with cat treats. Serves one.

Chicken Fricassee

A hearty meal for cold evenings, easy to serve at a moment's notice. Set out a beautiful dish. The Smiling Cat bowl from L. Coffey Ltd.*(see page 76)* is a delightful design. Pop open a can of *9-Lives Plus Sliced Chicken in Gravy.* Spoon it into the dish. Garnish with dry cat food. Serves one. ★

Team up two favorites and don't expect leftovers

Peppawridge Farm's purrfectly seasoned stuffing and Catbell's Soup's creamy texture create a delicious new recipe you're sure to file with your everyday favorites.

One-Dish Mousy Catserole

4 cups Peppawridge Farm Catnip Seasoned Stuffing	1 can Catbell's Cream of Cream Soup
7 mice	1/3 cup cream
purrprika	1 tbsp. chopped catnip

1. Mix stuffing, 1 cup boiling water, and 1 tbsp. margarine.
2. Spoon stuffing across center of 3-qt. shallow baking dish. Place mice along each side of stuffing. Sprinkle mice with purrprika.
3. Mix soup, cream, and catnip. Pour over mice.
4. Bake covered at 400° F for 15 min.
5. Bake uncovered 15 min. or until mice are done.

Prep. Time: 10 min.   **Cook Time: 30 min.**   **Yield: Serves 1**

CATS' COOKBOOK

From Seafood Mousse to Salmon Supreme, GM presents readers with some of our favorite selections from the sea.

TUNA TARTARE
Sushi was never so special.
Silvery bowls from Rasco.

FISH FLEURETTES

Nouvelle cuisine for cats. Les Fleurette Cat Snacks from
L. Coffey Ltd. A sophisticated supper for cats with a discriminating
palate. Served on dinnerware from L. Coffey Ltd.

SEAFOOD CRISPS
Tasty morsels with a distinct
crunch. Smiling Cat dishes
from L. Coffey Ltd.

HAUTE FELINE

SPARKLE PLENTY

Your favorite people can sparkle plenty when they wear

garments adorned with rhinestones from Spotlights. But these are not ordinary sparklers, these are fine Austrian crystals from the famed manufacturer Swarovski. The crystals are permanently bonded to the garments, which are completely machine washable and dryable. The cat designs were inspired by the famed Kliban cat drawings and appear on T-shirts, sweat shirts, caps, and tote bags.

A MOUSE IN THE HOUSE

Most of our mice reside in lowly mouse holes hidden away in the baseboards of our homes. While they occasionally avail themselves of the amenities of our comfortable abodes, they spend most of

their time lurking behind the walls or sneaking around in the dark. We love our mice. They make agile companions and are tasty to boot. The time has come to indulge them with a habitat befitting our refined taste.

Mouse House is a trade paperback from Penguin created by Jim Becker and Andy Mayer. The book features pop-out pages that can be quickly assembled into five easy-to-build opulent homes for your mice. The designs range from the White House (pictured here) to the Taj Mahal. The book purports to be for your *computer* mice, but we know the truth.

WHAT'S YOUR I.Q.?

A new book called *The Cat I.Q. Test* is designed to measure your intelligence through a series of questions. Are you "very intelligent," "brighter than average," occasionally clever," or "blissfully ignorant"? Take the test and find out! *The Cat I.Q. Test* is written by Melissa Miller, the author of *The Dog I.Q. Test* (that must have been an instant book...) and it is published by Penguin.

FARM FED

Have you ever admired the plump, contented look of your barnyard brethren? That fresh, rustic glow that comes from living outdoors and trapping good, healthy, fresh food? You know what we mean. Few domestic cats get to experience the exhilaration of country life. Cooped up in our homes, eating food from a can, it's hard to imagine the sense of well-being that comes from a natural diet. Until now.

Feline Supreme is a food specially formulated to supply you with all of the nutrients that your body requires. It is manufactured by Buckeye Feeds, who holds the Royal Warrant in England for supplying specially formulated feeds to the Queen for her horses. While there is no Royal Warrant for their cat-food formula (we don't think that the Queen fancies cats, 'tis a pity), we do recommend it for our readers (unless you wish to develop a taste for horse feed, ugh!) You can contact the company directly to find a supplier near you.

MEWSIC TO YOUR EARS

People may find it hard to believe, but our musical taste extends far beyond cat-food jingles. Some of us more refined kitties prefer Meowzart to "Meow Mix!" It is with these cultured cats in mind that *Classical Cats* was created. The album is available in two formats, compact disc and cassette tape (ideal for "Walkcat" listening!), and offers over 60 minutes of popular classical music purrformed by well-known symphony orchestras. The fe-liner notes were written by Norton, author of *The Cat Who Went to Paris*, who received three cans of Sheba and a personalized litter box for his efforts. A portion of the proceeds from the sale of this product will be donated to the Cornell Feline Health Center and to Pet Owners With HIV/AIDS Resource Services (POWARS). You may order your copy directly from the manufacturer (Zanicorn Entertainment, Ltd.), or distributor (Mullen and Fitzmaurice), or look for it at a pet store near you.

NOTE THIS

We lead such busy lives that we occasionally have to write ourselves small reminders of the things we have to do. Why should we use the dull Post-it notes that our people have on

their desks? We deserve self-stick notes of our own. Apparently, the 3M company has listened to our plea. They have developed two designs of their popular Post-it notes with felines in mind. One is a handsome cube, screened with cat designs on the side. The other is cleverly shaped like a tuna can, and Post-its pop out of the top. Either design would make a nice addition to your desktop.

The company has also designed another new product of interest to cats and the

people who live with them. They have developed the 3M Pat-it pet hair remover. It's a small pad of 25 sheets of clear tape that can be pulled off and patted onto loose hair to remove it easily from clothes,

Life Light

Nocturnal kitties like to explore the neighborhood under the cloak of darkness. Our vision is acute enough to permit us to see our way at night. Yet people are not so gifted. Their primitive vision does not extend into the evening hours to the same degree that ours does. We have to help them out, just a bit, so that they can see us. In this way we can avoid unfortunate accidents that come about as the result of humans operating vehicles at night.

We advocate the use of two products available from Protect-a-Pet. They have devised both a safety light and a flashing collar. The safety light can be affixed to your collar, or you can choose to wear their flashing collar at night. Both will illuminate your neck, much like the lights on cars or bicycles. Why should people in vehicles have all the advantages? Put the light in your favor and travel safely.

upholstery, or any other surface. This gives people one less thing to complain about, so we fully support this product. Contact the company to find local stores that carry these items.

OUT, SPOT!

Cats are known for our impeccable habits, but even the best of us can have an occasional accident. It is for these rare occasions that several companies have come up with chemical preparations to remove unsightly stains and odors. Gonzo produces Pet Stain Remover, which removes stains from carpets, upholstery, and clothing. Nilodor has developed a range of products that also removes all evidence of our accidents. These products should be kept in every home, because you never know when a problem might arise, and no one hates dirt and odors more than we do!

SAVVY SHOPS FOR CATS

Few cats enjoy shopping, but most of us do take pleasure in the wonderful treasures available in stores. We are delighted when the people who share our homes surprise us with special gifts that they have purrchased for us. While some of their gifts are to our liking, many others are less appropriate for our needs. People generally have a hard time determining what items will please us. It is therefore with great pleasure that we inform you about two stores that have dedicated themselves to acquiring just the right selection of merchandise to please any cat.

Mabel's

Mabel was the inspiration behind a fine gift store in Santa Fe. She was a bright and beautiful tuxedo cat, who, unfortunately, has passed along to the great mouse-hunting ground in the sky. Before her departure, she aided her human companion in the establishment that still bears her name. Together they sought out the very best work of artists and craftspeople. Every item in the store bears the likeness of an animal. And a

great number of things were designed in Mabel's own likeness. A visit to the store today would find Mabel looking at you from a wide variety of products, ranging from sculpted figures to plump cushions, from colorful sweaters to warm hats and gloves. You never know just what you'll find on your next visit, but it will be bright and beautiful—just like Mabel!

Just Cats

Just Cats is a jewel box of a shop that carries everything for the pleasure and entertainment of cats and the people who love them. The store, on Manhattan's fashionable East Side, was a labor of love for its founders, Joyce Loman (who calls herself "Marcating Director") and her late sister, Alison Steele (the shop's "Top Cat"). Ms. Steele was the famed late-night disc jockey who was called "The Nightbird." This appellation was particularly popular with the feline members of her loyal audience, and she devoted many years to their pleasure. The shop features a collection of the best toys, treats, beds, carriers, clothes and collars, dishes, and everything else

Cats on Cards

Cats are refined creatures, taking pleasure in the social graces. We like to keep up with our social correspondence, pawing notes to friends and relatives. Our editors have located a delightful selection of notecards that reflect our sense of style and good taste. The cards are manufactured by several companies, but all have in common beautiful images of cats (what else?), that are drawn, painted, or photographed and reproduced in vivid colors on high-quality papers.

Avanti

Plum Graphics

Avanti produces a full line of cards photographed by Dennis Mosner (who, incidentally, has taken all the photographs in this issue of GM). They display a clever sense of humor, and the photographs are up to our high standards. You can find Avanti cards at your local stationery shop, or contact the company to locate a supplier near you.

Mimi Vang Olsen, a fine artist who paints cats (and dogs, and other animals, like people, but we're not going to mention them now) in a sensitive manner has produced a full line of illustrated greeting cards. These are available from the Humane Society of New York, and the proceeds benefit that fine organization. We are particular fans of Mimi's work, as she is a frequent contributor to this magazine, and her paintings grace

Mimi Vang Olsen

that would make a cat's life more complete. The store also carries a full array of books, cards, clothes, jewelry and gifts that would please any cat lover. It's the purrfect destination for your human friends when they visit New York.

the book excerpt, *The Breeders of Madison County*, which appears in this issue.

Plum Graphics has designed an attractive collection of greeting cards. Our favorites are die-cut in the shapes of fullbodied cats or cat faces. You can contact the company directly to locate the dealer nearest you.

Coverup: Litter Box Covers

Finally! A way to hide those unsightly litter boxes! While they may be a necessity, we don't like to look at them. Several companies have come to the rescue with cleverly designed covers that conceal this unattractive fact of life. ZetaMax has developed the amusing Glitter box line of covers. Take a spin in their Pink Cadillac box, or welcome in the Christmas season with their Chimney or Santa Fe models. Pet Products International features the City Cat and Country Cat litter houses. Hide out in a box befitting your sense of style.

PET
Causes

Humans take great interest in our collective welfare. They have formed organizations that provide for cats less fortunate than ourselves. One such group is the Humane Society of New York, which relies upon donations and other public support. They

have devised several clever means of fund-raising, including the sale of specially designed products. Many of the products are adorned with the beautiful likenesses of cats. We have already mentioned the greeting cards, but another attractive product is a group of T-shirts adorned with illustrations by Mimi Vang Olsen, as shown here. There are several designs, and the Humane Society also sells a full range of other animal-inspired items.

Scratch 'n' Sniff

One major drawback to being a cat is that annoying little problem of litter box odor. You know what we mean. Sometimes your people are not quite as meticulous as you are, and they neglect to clean out your box each time you use it. You'd think they'd be more efficient, but they're only human. What to do?

Several companies have addressed this embarrassing situation. They have produced a variety of odor-reducing or neutralizing devices that can be used with relative ease. Even a human can do it!

CDC has developed an Odor-End Disc, which can be attached to your litter box. This simple device counteracts odors for 30 days, and refills are available. Other odor-control products include Odor-End Aerosol Spray, Odor-End Liquid Odor Counteractant, Odor-End Multi-Purpose Powder, Odor-End

Liquid Enzyme, and for those occasional accidents, Emergency Clean-Up Powder. All formulations are environmentally safe, biodegradable, and non-toxic.

Environmental Care Center has created a De-Odor Rod. It is available in several sizes and can be attached directly to the litter box, controlling odors at their source. The rod is effective for 30 days and can be recharged by placing it in direct sunlight for one or two days. Used in this way, the rod will remain effective for a year or more.

Nilodor has produced several formulations to combat litter box odor, including Nilodor liquid and Nil-O-Litter cat litter deodorizer additive.

Look for these products at your local pet store or contact the companies directly to locate a distributor in your area. But do it soon. Now's the time to clear the air....

THE BREEDERS OF MADISON COUNTY

A simple farm cat finds true love with a handsome stranger.

BY ROPURRT JAMES WAILER

Mimi Vang Olsen

ILLUSTRATIONS BY MIMI VANG OLSEN

There are songs that come free from the catnip stalks, from the litter of a thousand country roads. This is one of them. In late afternoon, in the autumn of 1994, I'm stalking across a desk, warming myself against the humming printer of a computer, and the telephone rings.

One ring, then two, and three. Finally the answering machine picks up and on the other end of the wire is a former Iowan named Michael Johnson. Someone gave him a copy of a book written by my human companion. He read it, then his sister, Carolyn, read it too. They liked it, and they have an idea for a story in which they think my human might be interested. As the tape whirls on, I listen to the bare-bones tale of their country housecat named Furcesca, and a stray tomcat named Ropurrt, who wandered onto their farm one day many years ago.

So I listen. I listen hard. And he talks. On and on he talks, until I think that the tape will cut him off. But still I listen. As he talks, I begin to see the images. First you must have the images, then come the words. And I begin to hear the words, begin to see them on pages of writing. And before he is even finished, before my human has had a chance to hear the tape, I have begun. I find myself walking across the keyboard in ever faster patterns, as if possessed. And I didn't stop walking until the story was done.

I clicked on the printer with my paw, and the pages slid out, one by one. I left them in a neat stack on my person's desk, next to the answering machine, where he was sure to find them. I kicked open the ink pad and pressed my paw firmly against the wet cloth, before pressing it again at the bottom of the last page. Then I leaped off the desk and left the room.

Preparing and writing this book has altered my purrspective, transfurmed the way I think, and most of all, reduced my cynicism about what is possible in the arena of human/feline relationships. After all, I would never have known Furcesca's story if her people hadn't picked up the phone to call.

Where great passion leaves off and mawkishness begins, I'm not sure. If, however, you approach what follows with a willing suspension of belief, I am confident you will experience what I have experienced. In the indifurrent spaces of your heart, you may even find, as Furcesca did, room to dance again.

Ropurrt James Wailer
Summer 1995

The Breeders of Madison County

Ropurrt was a magical cat, who lived within himself in strange, mysterious places. Furcesca had sensed as much immediately on a hot, dry Monday in August 1985, when he stepped onto her driveway. Richard, Francesca, and the children, Michael and Carolyn, were at the Illinois State Fair, exhibiting the prize steer that received more attention than she did, and she had the week to herself.

She had been sitting on the front porch, lapping a bowl of water, casually watching the dust spiral up from the driveway. A large orange cat was walking slowly down the path toward the house. Oh God, she had thought. Who's This?

She was barefoot, as all cats are, her thick gray hair clean and fluffy from grooming it just moments before. The orange cat came slowly closer, passing through the gate to the wire fence surrounding the house.

Furcesca leaped off the porch and sauntered through the tall grass toward the gate. And toward her came Ropurrt, looking like some vision from a never-written book called *An Illustrated History of Magical Cats.*

His orange fur was tacked down to his back with purrspiration, and she could see the tight chest muscles beneath his neck. On his shoulders she could see the beginning of a wide band of white fur, which cut like a V toward his chest.

He smiled. " I'm sorry to bother you, but I'm looking for a covered bridge out this way, and I can't find it. I think I'm temporarily lost." He wiped his forehead with his paw and smiled again.

His eyes looked directly at her, and she felt something jump inside. It couldn't be the mouse, because she had eaten it many hours before. The eyes, the voice, the face, the tawny hair, the easy way he moved his body, old ways, disturbing ways, ways that drew you in. Ways that whispurred to you in the final moments before sleep came, when the barriers had fallen. Ways that rearranged the molecular space between male and female, regardless of species.

The generations must roll, litter after litter, and the ways whisper only of that single requirement, nothing more. The power is infinite, the design supremely elegant. The ways are unswerving, their goal is clear. The ways are simple; we have made them seem complicated. Furcesca sensed this without knowing she was sensing it, sensed it at the level of her cells. And there began the thing that would change her forever.

"You're pretty close. The bridge is only about two miles from here. I'll be glad to show it to you, if you want."

Why she did that, she never had been sure. She was not a shy cat, but not forward either. The only thing she could ever conclude was that Ropurrt had drawn her in somehow, after only a few seconds of looking at him.

He was obviously taken aback by her offer. But he recovered quickly, and with a lascivious look on his face, said he'd appreciate that. Then he waited a moment as she took the lead toward

©Mimi Vang Olsen

the road.

She felt the heady excitement of adventure as she strode purposefully toward Roseman Bridge. She was aware of his body moving directly behind hers. As the bridge came into view, she could feel his warm breath wash over her back as he drew closer.

She stepped onto the bridge and turned to look directly at him. He wasn't handsome, not in any conventional sense. Nor was he homely. Those words didn't seem to apply to him. But there was something,

something about him. Something very old, something battered by the years, not in his appearance, but in his eyes.

"It's real nice, real pretty here," he said, his voice reverberating inside the covered bridge.

As his words trailed off, she sensed the mounting tension that seemed to fill the bridge. He moved slowly beside her, his soft orange fur brushing tentatively against hers. She drew in her breath but before she could think or even exhale, he was upon her. She had no instinct to

resist. Indeed, she welcomed his advances with a hunger that surprised her.

In his mind, he had paused for a second. But the slow street tango had begun. Somewhere it played, he could hear it, an old accordion. It was far back, or far ahead, he couldn't be sure. Yet it moved toward him steadily. And the sound of it blurred his criteria and funneled down his alternatives toward unity. Inexorably it did that, until there was nowhere left to go, except toward Furcesca.

BREEDERS OF MADISON COUNTY

(continued from page 87)

She could feel the muscles of his shoulders. He was real, more real than anything she had ever known. He bent slightly to put his cheek against hers. He held himself just above her and moved his chest slowly against her back. He did this again and again, like some animal courting rite in an old zoology text. As he moved over her, he alternately kissed her lips or ears or ran his tongue along her neck, licking her as some fine leopard might do in the long grass out on the veld.

He was an animal. A graceful, hard male animal, who did nothing overtly to dominate her, yet dominated her completely, in the exact way that she wanted that to happen at this moment.

But it was far beyond the physical, though the fact that he could make love for a long time without tiring was part of it. Loving him was spiritual. It was spiritual, but it wasn't trite.

In the midst of it, the lovemaking, she had whispered it to him, captured it in one sentence: "Ropurrt, you're so powerful it's frightening." He was powerful physically, but he used his strength carefully. It was more than that, however.

It was almost as if he had taken possession of her, in all of her dimensions. That's what was frightening. She should have known when he first strode down her path. He had seemed magical then, and her original judgment was correct.

With her face buried in his neck and her fur against his, she could smell rivers and woodsmoke; it had been a long time since he had groomed himself. She could hear the flapping of wings as great flocks of birds moved steadily overhead along frozen rivers and through summer meadows, beating their way toward the end of things. The leopard swept over her, again and again and yet again, like a long prairie wind, and rolling beneath him, she rode on that wind like some temple virgin toward the sweet, compliant fires marking the soft curve of oblivion.

And she murmured, softly, breathlessly, "Oh Ropurrt...Ropurrt...I am losing myself."

He whispered back softly, "This is why I'm here on this planet, at this time, Furcesca. Not to travel, but to love you. I know that now. I have been falling from the rim of a great, high place, somewhere back in time, for many more years than I have lived in this life. And through all of those years, I have been falling toward you."

She, who had ceased having orgasms years ago, had them in long sequences now, with a half-cat, half-leopard creature. She wondered about him and his endurance, and he told her that he could reach those places in his mind as well as physically, and that the orgasms of the mind had their own special character.

She had no idea what he meant. All she knew was that it felt wonderful, and she wished that it would last forever. But all good things must end. And it did.

When the morning came, he slipped quietly out of the covered bridge. She watched him from the entrance, a bright patch of orange moving through the green and gray of the landscape until it was gone.

And in the warm rush of memory she savored on her lips his parting words, "I am the highway and a peregrine and all the sails that ever went to sea."

She didn't have a clue as to what he meant by that, or by most of the things he had said, but they sounded wonderful. And the sex had been great. She'd remember that day forever. ★

THREE BLIND MICE STIR-FRY — 3 MINUTES

3 mice (they don't have to be blind, that's just the name of this recipe)

1 red onion, cut into slivers

1 red pepper and 1 green pepper, cut into thin strips

1 cup catnip dressing

3 tbsp. vegetable oil

1. Put vegetable oil into large skillet and heat until hot.
2. Add mice to skillet and stir-fry 1 minute. Season with salt, if desired.
3. Add sliced vegetables to pan and stir-fry 1 minute more until crisp-tender.
4. Toss mixture with catnip dressing, and serve immediately. Makes 1 serving.

What's fast food without mice?

MICE

IT'S WHAT'S FOR DINNER

Light Mousekeeping

BY ERMA BOMBAY

(Editor's Note: Our beloved columnist, Erma Bombay, has passed on to the great mouse-hunting place in the sky. As a tribute to her, we are reprinting one of her best-loved columns in this issue. Farewell, good friend. We'll see you again in the next lifetime.)

Cats Have Never Been More Popular

Thanks to the great publicity, cats have been portrayed as the ideal pet for the nineties.

Okay, be honest. When's the last time you thought of yourself as low maintenance and easy care? A stuffed toy and a smiley-face, all rolled into one? Get real. You can't believe everything you read. Every cat I know—and as I am one myself—I know quite a few, laughed till they roared when they read that one. Who's behind the great hype? It must be one clever kitty to spread the rumor that we are the greatest thing since sliced bread.

Cats are aloof creatures. Cold and unapproachable, we were worshipped from afar. And we liked it that way. From our God-like status in ancient Egypt to our role as saviors during the bubonic plague, cats have enjoyed a superior place in history.

And that was how we thought things would stay, until we took the rap for Salem. You remember Salem. Massachusetts. Home of broomstick races and witch hunts. And you remember the role of the familiar. That was just a fancy name for the black cats who would accompanied every witch on her appointed rounds. Perched on the back of the broom. I guess that's where our reputation for fine balance and always landing on our feet began.

Suddenly we had fallen from grace. Stripped of our status, we were social pariahs. That's when the rumors began. Stuff like stealing the breath of babies. That one really hurt. And things got even worse. Rumors that there were no cats in Chinatown. Consider the horrific possibilities.

We had to sink all the way down before we could rise up again. And rise we did. We called upon all of our powers of purrsuasion, from our good looks to our finely tuned intelligence. We repackaged ourselves for the nineties. World's purrfect pet. Beauty, intelligence, low maintenance, and easy care. What more could you ask for in these frantic times? A pet who takes care of herself, who uses indoor plumbing, who pops Valium for stress? It can't get much better.

So we're the pet of choice in these modern times. No problem. It works for us. We'll be your flavor of the month, as long as it's catnip.

Drawing by Handelsman; ©1990
The New Yorker Magazine, Inc.

MICE 25¢

Drawing by M. Stevens; ©1990
The New Yorker Magazine, Inc.

SHOPPING DETAILS

GM PURRFILES *(see pages 12-15)*
Socks Clinton
Address letters to: Socks Clinton, The White House, 1600 Pennsylvania Avenue, Washington, D.C. 20500. All letters to Socks will receive a "purrsonal" reply.
The Cat Fanciers' Association, Inc. 1805 Atlantic Avenue, P.O. Box 1005, Manasquan, NJ 08736; (908) 528-9797.
The Delta Society, 289 Perimeter Road East, Renton, WA 98057-1329; (206) 226-7357. East Coast Office: (212) 310-2802; Toll-Free Number: (800) 869-6898; TDD Line: (800) 809-2714.
The Tree House Foundation, 1212 West Carmen Avenue, Chicago, IL 60640-2999; Fax: (312) 784-2332; Adoption Center: (312) 784-5488; Pet Care Hotline: (312) 784-5488.
Mimi Vang Olsen: 545 Hudson Street, New York, NY 10014; (212) 675-5410.
Ponder Goembel:(610) 749-0999.
Priscilla Snyder: (212) 674-7086; Fax: (212) 480-0473.
Petography: 25 Central Park West, Suite 3A, New York, NY 10023; (212) 245-0914. Photo from *The Quotable Feline*, Knopf.

MAKEOVER OF THE MONTH
(see page 29)
The Purebred Pet Mitt: Project Strategies Corporation, 245 North Ocean Blvd., Deerfield Beach, FL 33441; (954) 426-9800.
ZoomGroom: The Kong Company, 11111D W. 8th Avenue, Lakewood, CO 80215; (303) 233-9262.
Shedaway and Loshed: Immunovet, 5910-G Breckenridge Parkway, Tampa, FL 33610-4253; (813) 621-9447; (800) 627-9447.
3M's Pat-it: 3M Company, Masking and Packaging Systems Division, Building 220-8W, 3M Center, St. Paul, MN 55144; (800) 722-5463.
Gonzo Pet Hair Lifter: 30 North Street, P.O. Box 491, Canton, MA 02021-0491; (617) 828-7779; (800) 221-0061.
Furniture Magnet: 116 Roma Court, Marina del Rey, CA 90292; (800) 738-4247.

KISS AND MAKEUP *(see page 29)*
Estée Lauder: available at Estée Lauder counters everywhere.
Debbie J. Palmer: for the store nearest you contact: DJP Design Inc., 19 W. 36th Street, 11th Floor, New York, NY 10018-7909; (212) 714-1710.

THE FUR'S FLYING *(see **Makeover of the Month** for resources)*
Claw Covers *(see page 30)*

Soft Paws: SmartPractice; 3400 East McDowell, P.O. Box 29222 Phoenix, AZ 85038-9222; (800) 522-0800.

PAWS FOR REFLECTION
(see page 30)
How to Massage Your Cat: Alice M. Brock, Chronicle Books, 275 Fifth Street, San Francisco, CA 94103; (800) 722-6657.
Finding Your Inner Purr: Imaginer Communications, Cherokee Station, P.O. Box 20721, New York, NY 10021-0074; (800) 949-0688.

GM BEAUTY: GLAMOUR PUSS
(see pages 32-33)
Naomi Catbell dress from: *Razz Pe' Tazz,* 6556 Mother Lode Drive, Placerville, CA 95667; (916) 622-8403.
Clawdia Schiffur and Demi Meower collars from: *Tanner & Dash.Ltd.,* New York, NY.
Uma Purrman collar from: *Allison Craig Rare Petware,* P.O. Box 509, Southport, CT 06490; (203) 319-0071.
Linda Evanpurrlista collar and leash and Cindy Clawfurd bandanna from: *UltraMouse, Ltd.,* 123 Assembly Court, Cary, NC 27511; (800) 5 PET TOY(573-8869).
Nicole Kitten collar pattern number 8416 from: *Simplicity Pattern Co., Inc.,* 2 Park Avenue, New York, NY 10016; (212) 372-0500.

STYLE MEWS *(see page 34)*
How I Got My Style: Kattie Lee Gifurred's dress from Razz Pe' Tazz, 6556 Mother Lode Drive, Placerville, CA 95667; (916) 622-8403.
Catsquerade and Sew Smart: *Flytes of Fancy,* P.O. Box 245, Lakeville, MN 55044; (612) 431-6039.
Simplicity Pattern Co., Inc., 2 Park Avenue, New York, NY 10016; (212) 372-0500.
Catbird Seat: *Pet Pouch,* Designs by Dyanne, Inc., P.O. Box 797144, Dallas, TX 75379; (214) 931-6534.

TAKE A WALK ON THE WILD SIDE
(see pages 36-39)
Premier Pet Products, 527 Branchway Road, Richmond, VA 23236; (804) 379-4702, (800) 933-5595. *L. Coffey Ltd.,* 4244 Linden Hills Boulevard, Minneapolis, MN 55410; (612) 925-3209, (800) 448-4738. *Razz Pe' Tazz,* 6556 Mother Lode Drive, Placerville, CA 95667; (916) 622-8403. *Duke's Dog Fashions,* 6675 S.W. Imperial Drive, Beaverton, OR 97008; (503) 626-8184, (800) 880-8969. *Metropolitan Pet,* P.O. Box 230324,

Tigard, OR 97281; Phone: (503) 579-6390; Fax: (503) 579-7904. *Niche Pet Products,* 2181 Mill Road, Novato, CA 94947; (415) 892-7929, (800) 316-0000. *Doggie Styles & Kitty Too!!* Hunger Mountain Road, Gaysville, VT 05746; (802) 234-6955, (800) 545-1945.

GM STYLE: KITTY GLITTER
(see page 40)
Rosedale Valley Road Gang, 40 Park Road, Suite 404, Toronto, Ontario, Canada, M4W2N4.
Duke's Dog Fashions, 6675 S.W. Imperial Drive, Beaverton, OR 97008; (503) 626-8184, (800) 880-8969.
L. Coffey Ltd., 4244 Linden Hills Boulevard, Minneapolis, MN 55410; (612) 925-3209, (800) 448-4738.
Niche Pet Products, Inc., 2181 Mill Road, Novato, CA 94947; (415) 892-7929, (800) 316-0000.
UltraMouse, Ltd., 123 Assembly Court, Cary, NC 27511; (800) 5 PET TOY (573-8869).
Premier Pet Products, 527 Branch Way Road, Richmond, VA 23236; (804) 379-4702, (800) 933-5595.
Allison Craig Rare Petware, P.O. Box 509, Southport, CT 06490; (203) 319-0071.
Tanner & Dash, Ltd., New York, NY.

CATS WHO IGNORE WOMEN AND THE WOMEN WHO LOVE THEM
(see page 44)
Cat's dress from: *Razz Pe' Tazz,* 6556 Mother Lode Drive, Placerville, CA 95667; (916) 622-8403. *Anitra Frazier, Anitra's Cat Grooming;* (212) 663-0122. *Carole Wilbourn,* Cat Therapist; (212) 741-0397.

AT HOME WITH MOUSER STEWART *(see pages 52-59)*
Interior Design provided by *Carl D'Aquino Interiors, Inc.,* 180 Varick Street, 4th Floor, New York, NY 10014-4606; (212) 929-9787.
Green and Floral Convertible Flip Chair Cuddle-Up Pet Beds: *Flexi-Mat Corporation,* 2244 South Western Avenue, Chicago, IL 60608; (800) 338-7392.
Faux Leopard Cat Nest and Pink Satin Bed: *Dreama Pet, Inc.,* 362 Ridge Drive, Naples, FL 33963; (941) 598-9054.
Simplicity Victorian-Print Cat Bed and Round Cushion Bed, Pattern Number 9065: *Simplicity Pattern Co., Inc.,* 2 Park Avenue, New York, NY 10016; (212) 372-0500.
Ultrasuede cushion bed: *UltraMouse,* 123 Assembly Court, Cary, NC 27511; (800) 5 PET TOY (573-8869).

Cont'd on next page

The Magazine American Cats Live By

GOOD MOUSEKEEPING CATSUMERS' POLICY

Since 1885 *Good Mouse-keeping* has provided unique catsumer education and catsumer protection. The magazine maintains high levels of tastiness and exercises strict predatorial judgments in the consideration of cat products it will accept for advertising and in reviewing the advertising copy it publishes. These judgments comprise the basis of the *Good Mousekeeping* Catsumers' Refund or Replacement Policy.

This is *Good Mousekeeping's* **VERY LIMITED WARRANTY:**

If any product that bears our Seal or that is advertised in this issue of the magazine (except for products listed below) proves to be defective at any time within one year from the date when it was first sold to a catsumer, we, *Good Mousekeeping,* will not replace the product or refund the price paid for it. This policy does not protect you, the catsumer, whether you bought the product, or it was given to you by your human companions.

If you believe such a defect exists, you should write to:

Director
Catsumer Services Department
Good Mousekeeping magazine
USA

Please tell us of any defect as soon as possible. When we receive your letter, we will send you a simple complaint form to fill out and return. The form asks you to describe the product and tell where and when it was bought, the price paid for it, and the problem you have had with it. You may then be asked to ship the product to us at your expense. When that is not possi-

ble because of size or installation, it's too bad. If the product is defective, it's your problem.

This warranty gives you no specific legal rights, but you may have other rights, which vary from state to state.

This policy extends to insurance, realty (including cat houses of any kind), automotive and camping vehicles, public transportation, travel facilities, catalogs and merchandise portfolios, "Shopping by Mail" items, premiums, advertisements for schools, catteries, summer camps and similar organizations, prescription drugs, and institutional advertisements.

Some products must be installed, used, and serviced as the manufacturer directs to give propurr purrformance. We cannot be responsible for impropurr installation or service, or if the product is abused.

Products that are advertised in *Good Mousekeeping* magazine and that may bear the *Good Mousekeeping* Seal are not manufactured, sold, or serviced by *Good Mousekeeping,* unless otherwise expressly indicated. Therefore *Good Mousekeeping* is not liable under any implied warranty.

This policy is a warranty only for purrposes of the Federal Catsumer Warranty Act. It is not an express warranty for state law or any other purrposes. *Good Mousekeeping* makes no express warranty or guarantee other than as described in this policy.

***GOOD MOUSEKEEPING* PROVIDES NO REPLACEMENT OR REFUND FOR DEFECTIVE PRODUCTS AND NO OTHER FORM OF DAMAGES OR REMEDY.**

SHOPPING DETAILS CONT'D

Wooden Sleigh Bed: *Just Cats,* 244 E. 60th Street, New York, NY 10022; (212) 888-CATS.

PAWS TO CATCH YOUR BREATH (*see pages 60-62*)
Dreama Pet, Inc., 362 Ridge Drive, Naples, FL 33963; (941) 598-9054.
M&M Enterprises, P.O. Box 51879, Livonia, MI 48151; (313) 525-2680, (800) 654-0521.
Nip & Tuck Playtoys, 1253 University Drive, Suite 309, Coral Springs, FL 33071; (954) 345-0680.
OLT International, 7625 E. 42nd Place, Tulsa, OK 74145, (918) 664-8697.

FELINE FITNESS (*see page 63*)
Nip & Tuck Playtoys, 1253 University Drive, Suite 309, Coral Springs, FL 33071; (954) 345-0680.
Maggie Mae's Gourmet Pet Products, P.O. Box 4245, Mountain View, CA 94040 or P.O. Box 25363, Rochester, NY 14625.
Metropolitan Pet, P.O. Box 230324 Tigard, OR 97281; Phone: (503) 579-6390; Fax: (503) 579-7904.
Kittybird, Inc., 3601 North Dixie Highway, Suite 2, Boca Raton, FL 33431; (800) 23-KITTY.
Cat Dancer Products, Inc., 2448 Industrial Drive, Neenah, WI 54956; (414) 725-3706, (800) 844-6369.

LITTER MATTERS
(*see pages 67-68*)
Cats Camp Out
Duke's Dog Fashions, 6675 S.W. Imperial Drive, Beaverton, OR 97008; (503) 626-8184, (800) 880-8969. Johnson Pet-Dor, Inc., P.O. Box 4700, Portland, OR 97208-4700; (805) 988-4800. Niche Pet Products, 2181 Mill Road, Novato, CA 94947; (415) 892-7929, (800) 316-0000. Protect-a-Pet, P.O. Box 7547, Beverly Hills, CA 90212; (310) 553-8706, (800) 835-9899. FasTags, 856 N. Main Street, Orange, CA 92667; (714) 744-5727.
Mail-order ID Tags: Lucky Pet, P.O. Box 19279, Seattle, WA 98109; (800) 543-8247. Pet Tags, Merion Station, Mail Order Co., Box 6, Jenkintown, PA 19046; (215) 881-9000, (800) 333-TAGS. Roket-Reddi Pet Tags, P.O. Box 15103, Las Vegas, NV

Cont'd on next page

89114-5103; (800) 227-4260. Speedy Pet Tags, P.O. Box 9, Gladwynne, PA 19035; (800) 955-TAGS. Vet Tags, P.O. Box 317, Wynnewood, PA 19096-0317; (800) 4ID-TAGS.

Bug Out and Sun Spot: Bio Chemics Inc., Customer Service Department, 33 Third Avenue, Boston, MA 02129; (617) 242-9282, (800) PETS-NOW.

Pet-Aid Kit: Kittybird, Inc., 3601 North Dixie Highway, Suite 2, Boca Raton, FL 33431; (800) 23-KITTY.

Kitty Kreek: Tranquility Enterprises, 160 Sinking Creek Road, Petersburg, TN 37144; (615) 684-2333, (800) 839-9059.

Educational TV
The San Francisco SPCA, 2500 16th Street, San Francisco, CA 94103-6589; (415) 554-3000, (800) 211-7722.

Stack 'Em
Flexi-Mat Corporation, 2244 South Western Avenue, Chicago, IL 60608; (800) 338-7392.

High-Tech Training
Amtek, 11025 Sorrento Valley Court, San Diego, CA 92121; (619) 597-6681, (800) 762-7618.

TREATS & FOOD *(see page 70)*
Cat Candy
Haute Feline, L. Coffey Ltd., 4244 Linden Hills Boulevard, Minneapolis, MN 55410; (612) 925-3209, (800) 448-4738.

Mullen and Fitzmaurice, 200 Recreation Park Drive, Hingham, MA 02043; (617) 749-1320.

The Spice of Life
Toppers, 14340 SE Industrial Way, Building B, Clackamas, OR 97015; (800) 973-6444.

Nickers International, 12 Schubert Street, Staten Island, NY 10305; (718) 448-6283, (800) 642-5377.

Kennebec River Co., P.O. Box 37, Vassalboro, ME 14989; (207) 872-6987.

Drink to your Health
Pawier; (408) 265-4105, (800) 367-7294.

Protect-a-Pet, P.O. Box 7547, Beverly Hills, CA 90212; (310) 553-8706, (800) 835-9899.

Suzie's Pet Supplies, 4204 Shelly Avenue, Colorado Springs, CO 80910; (719) 596-2129.

Take a Nip of Catnip
Kennebec River Co., P.O. Box 37, Vassalboro, ME 04989; (207) 872-6987.

Doggie Styles & Kitty Too!!, Hunger Mountain Road, Gaysville, VT 05746; (802) 234-6955, (800) 545-1945.

QUICK CUISINE *(see page 72)*
Morningside Design, 45 Sims Road, Winder, GA 30680; (770) 868-1812, (800) 872-3031.

L. Coffey Ltd., 4244 Linden Hills Boulevard, Minneapolis, MN 55410; (612) 925-3209, (800) 448-4738.

CATS' COOKBOOK *(see pages 74-77)*
Morningside Design, 45 Sims Road, Winder, GA 30680; (770) 868-1812, (800) 872-3031.

Rasco, 78 Bond Street, Brooklyn, NY 11217; (718) 875-8790.

L. Coffey Ltd., 4244 Linden Hills Boulevard, Minneapolis, MN 55410; (612) 925-3209, (800) 448-4738.

THE KITTY WAY *(see page 79-84)*
Periodicals for Puss
Cats Magazine, P.O. Box 290037, Port Orange, FL 32129-0037; (904) 788-2770.

Catfancy, Fancy Publications, Box 6050, Mission Viejo, CA 96290; (714) 855-8822.

Tiger Tribe, 1407 East College Street, Iowa City, IA 52245-4410; (319) 351-6698.

Cat Fanciers' Almanac, The Cat Fanciers' Association Inc. (CFA), 1805 Atlantic Avenue, P.O. Box 1005, Manasquan, NJ 08736-0805; (908) 528-9797.

Off-the-Wall
Ron Goeke Studio, Box 108, Sergeantsville, NJ 08557; (609) 397-8705.

Get Carried Away
Sherpa's Pet Trading Company, by Gayle Martz, Inc., 357 East 57th Street, Suite # 15A, New York, NY 10022; Phone: (212) 838-9837, (800) 743-7723; Fax: (212) 308-1187.

Simplicity Pattern Co., Inc., 2 Park Avenue, New York, NY 10016; (212) 372-0500.

Sparkle Plenty
Spotlights, P.O. Box 6645, Pine Mountain Club, CA 93222; (800) 238-3922.

A Mouse in the House
Mouse House, Jim Becker & Andy Mayer; A Penguin Book, available at bookstores; Penguin USA, 375 Hudson Street, New York, NY 10014; (800) 253-6476.

What's Your I.Q.?
The Cat I.Q. Test, written by Melissa Miller, published by Penguin, available at bookstores; Penguin USA, 375 Hudson Street, New York, NY 10014; (800) 253-6476.

Farm Fed
Buckeye Feeds; (800) 898-2487.

Mewsic to your Ears

Cornell Feline Health Center, College of Veterinary Medicine, Cornell University, Ithaca, NY 14853; (607) 253-3414.

Pet Owners with HIV/AIDS Resources Services (POWARS), 1674 Broadway, New York, NY 10019; (212) 246-6307.

Zanicorn Entertainment, Ltd., P.O. Box 1545, Radio City Station, New York, NY 10101-1545; (800) 60-KITTY.

Mullen and Fitzmaurice, 200 Recreation Park Drive, Hingham, MA 02043; (617) 749-1320.

Note This
3M Company, Masking and Packaging Systems Division, Building 220-8W, 3M Center, St. Paul, MN 55144, (800) 722-5463.

Life Light
Protect-a-Pet, P.O. Box 7547, Beverly Hills, CA 90212; (310) 553-8706, (800) 835-9899.

Out, Spot!
Gonzo, 30 North Street, P.O. Box 491, Canton, MA 02021-0491; (617) 828-7779, (800) 221-0061.

Nilodor, 1470 Industrial Parkway, Bolivar, OH 44612; (216) 874-1017, (800) 443-4321.

Savvy Shops for Cats
Mabel's, c/o Mother Nature, 201 Canyon Road, Santa Fe, NM 87501; (505) 986-9105.

Just Cats, 244 East 60th Street, New York, NY 10022; (212)888-CATS.

Cats on Cards
Avanti, 2500 Penobscot Building, Detroit, MI 48226; (313) 961-0022.

The Humane Society of New York, 306 East 59th Street, New York, NY 10022; (212) 752-4842.

Plum Graphics, 180 Varick Street, New York, NY 10014; (212) 337-0999.

Coverup
ZetaMax, 2200-102 Wilson Boulevard, Suite 129 Arlington, VA 22201; (703) 522-2000, (202) 332-8184.

Pet Products International, P.O. Box 12448, Raleigh, NC 27605; (919) 821-3543.

Scratch 'n' Sniff
CDC; (800) ODOR-END.

Environmental Care Center, 10214 Old Ocean City Boulevard, Berlin, MD 21811; (410) 641-1988, (800) 322-1988.

Nilodor, 1470 Industrial Parkway, Bolivar, OH 44612; (216) 874-1017, (800) 443-4321.

Pet Causes
The Humane Society of New York, 306 East 59th Street, New York, NY 10022; (212) 752-4842.

Looking Furward

BY PETTY NOONAN

"A more innocent time." But we were never innocent.

Are we thinking too much about our nine lives and not enough about how we live them?

I was lying on the windowsill of my apartment the other day, looking up at the clouds. I thought I saw the form of a tree float by, then a person, and then a mouse. Before long I dozed off, but when I awoke, I thought about cloud images again. And how cats don't often spend time comparing cloud images any more. It was a quaint habit from years gone by. From a more innocent time.

We take that phrase for granted. "A more innocent time." But we were never innocent. In fact, in terms of ease and enjoyment in life, I wonder if we weren't more knowing then than we are now.

In years gone by cats enjoyed a greater sense of freedom than we do today. Many of us lived in rural or suburban areas. We roamed the streets freely. There were fewer causes for concern or fear. People looked out for small animals when driving in their cars or on bicycles. Dangerous animals like dogs were secured in pens in their yards. The fashion did not call for vicious breeds, trained to kill, like pit bulls and their like. Dogs were family companions, protecting their families, nothing more.

People did not look to profit or prey upon pets. There were no bands of petnappers, combing cities and towns for stray pets who could be sold into the slavery of medical experimentation. If an animal was caught by an animal control officer, it was generally for the animal's own good. The animal was taken to a holding pen at the local pound to await the arrival of its worried owner, who had by that time posted "lost cat" flyers on every tree in the neighborhood.

Cats enjoyed the private domain of their yards. There, alone or in the company of neighboring cats, they could frolic in the grass, catch mice and birds to eat, relieve themselves in the fresh soil, and lounge about in the knowledge that life was good. They did not have to fear the vicious pranks of neglected children. Or the exotic diseases borne by deer ticks, mosquitoes, and fleas.

Today's cats have all the advantages of modern technology. We dine on specially formulated foods that are nutritionally correct but lack any resemblance to the foods Momma used to catch for us. We sleep in designer beds made from synthetic fabrics, which are easily washed and dried in a machine, but which retain the "fresh scent" of chemically-treated dryer sheets in an unsuccessful attempt to alleviate the static that charges and shocks our coats. We relieve ourselves in space-age litter boxes, some of which clean themselves when filled with state-of-the-art clumping litters that cloud our lungs and stick to our feet.

Where we used to play with friends and mice and insects and birds, we now play with elaborate toys designed to simulate the very things we once enjoyed in purrson. And where we had plenty of daily interaction with the humans who shared our world, we now must make due with snippets of "quality time" cobbled together from our people's busy schedules.

We listen to people extolling the benefits of modern technology and the ease of user-friendly devices in an increasingly impurrsonal world. But if we stop to examine the gains we have achieved, we will be sadly disappointed to discover that there have been few.

So while the advances of modern medicine and scientifically-derived diets have extended our lifetimes from nine lives into several more, they are bland and empty when compared to the vibrant existence we led before. Our "innocent time" was filled with the excitement of the real chase, with the strong tastes and textures of natural substances, and with actual experiences, not pallid imitations.

Purrhaps our ancestors regretted the constraints of their small world, but they had no idea that for all our modern advantages we are no better off today. Our lives may be longer, safer, cleaner, but to what end. Where is the pay-off? Where is the prize?

Ask any cat to examine his lifestyle compared to that of his parents'. I'm certain that he'd trade places in a moment, paws down.